always up to date

The law changes, but Nolo is always on top of it! We offer several ways to make sure you and your Nolo products are always up to date:

1 **Nolo's Legal Updater**

We'll send you an email whenever a new edition of your book is published! Sign up at **www.nolo.com/legalupdater**.

2 **Updates @ Nolo.com**

Check **www.nolo.com/update** to find recent changes in the law that affect the current edition of your book.

3 **Nolo Customer Service**

To make sure that this edition of the book is the most recent one, call us at **800-728-3555** and ask one of our friendly customer service representatives. Or find out at **www.nolo.com**.

The
Job Description
Handbook

by Margie Mader-Clark

FIRST EDITION	JANUARY 2006
Editor	LISA GUERIN
Cover Design	SUSAN PUTNEY
Book Design	SUSAN PUTNEY
Index	KATHERINE JENSEN
Proofreading	ROBERT WELLS
Printing	DELTA PRINTING SOLUTIONS, INC.

Mader-Clark, Marjorie.
   The job description handbook / Marjorie Mader-Clark.-- 1st ed.
     p. cm.
   ISBN 1-4133-0442-7 (alk. paper)
    1. Job descriptions--Handbooks, manuals, etc. 2. Personnel management--Handbooks, manuals, etc. I. Title.

HF5549.5.J613M33 2006
658.3'06--dc22

                                                 2005054706

Quantity sales: For information on bulk purchases or corporate premium sales, please contact the Special Sales Department. For academic sales or textbook adoptions, ask for Academic Sales. Call 800-955-4775 or write to Nolo, 950 Parker Street, Berkeley, CA 94710.

Acknowledgments

As a first-time author, my only experience with editors came when I read other peoples' acknowledgments. I truly did not know what to expect—enter Lisa Guerin. Lisa's role was simple; take everything I actually wrote and turn it into what I meant to say, let me know gently when I was nonsensical ("What do you mean here, Margie?"), remove grave errors, add knowledge where there was previously little, and make me a better writer. Thank you, Lisa, for your guidance and wisdom throughout this process.

Many thanks to Sigrid Metson of Nolo, for taking a leap with me and making this whole thing happen. Thanks also to Christi Dunlap, HR Consultant extraordinaire, for your help with the training piece. Thanks to the Burlingame Public Library for your chair, outlet, and internet connection, and thanks to Diet Coke and Ho-Hos for your fuel. I swear I didn't eat and drink in the library, because that's wrong.

Lastly, for the love, grace, and humor in my life, thanks to Austin and Calvin, my beloved little family.

About the Author

Author Margie Mader-Clark has been in the highest levels of the HR profession for more than 15 years, primarily in the fast-paced world of the Silicon Valley. She has experienced firsthand the power of good management—and sadly, the potentially devastating impact of poor management. She practices a simple, commonsense approach in her work in human resources. Time and again, employees leave companies because of unclear expectations, unfulfilled career opportunities, or lack of advancement. A good hire is the best foundation for a long and positive employment relationship, but clear communication and performance management also play an important role. And the basis of good hiring and managing is communicating exactly what the position entails, starting with the job description. Mader-Clark has implemented and taught these basic principles in companies like Netscape, Hyperion Solutions, and a number of Internet start-ups.

Table of Contents

Introduction

1 An Overview of Job Descriptions

2 Avoiding Legal Pitfalls

3 Analyze and Define the Job

4 Writing the Job Description

5 Using Job Descriptions

6 Troubleshooting

APPENDIX

A How to Use the CD-ROM

APPENDIX

B Tools and Checklists

APPENDIX

C Sample Job Descriptions

APPENDIX

D Laws and Agencies

Index

Introduction

Yₒu've probably picked up this book because you're getting ready to create a new position or make some managerial changes. Maybe you finally got approval to hire someone or you have to replace an employee who quit or was promoted out of your group. Perhaps you need to communicate your expectations to an employee who is having performance problems or let a star performer know what it will take to climb the company ladder. In all of these situations, your next step should be the same: to create or update a job description.

Writing job descriptions is one of those tasks managers tend to put off or handle half-heartedly, by continuing to use outdated descriptions or grabbing a generic template off the Internet. In the crush of day-to-day deadlines and emergencies, it can be hard to find the time for what might appear to be an exercise in paperwork. But carefully drafted job descriptions aren't just pieces of paper: They are the cornerstone to hiring effectively, communicating expectations, evaluating performance, terminating employees who can't meet your job requirements, and much more—all while keeping you and your company out of potential legal trouble.

The process of creating a job description may also offer a rare opportunity to examine your team and your company as a whole, and consider what human resources you will need to succeed. Where are you now? Where would you like to be in the future? And what kinds of skills and abilities will your people need to help get your company from here to there? A carefully drafted job description positions and prepares your group for the future.

What Is a Job Description?

A job description is simply a clear, concise depiction of a job's duties and requirements. Job descriptions can take many forms, but they typically have at least four parts:

- A job summary—an overview of the position, with a brief description of the most important functions. Because this will be the first thing applicants read, it's a great place to sell the job to the candidates you're trying to attract (and to weed out those who won't be able to meet your expectations).
- A list of job functions—a more detailed description of duties. While listing what people have to do to perform a job might seem pretty straightforward, it can be a legal minefield for managers who aren't aware of federal and state antidiscrimination laws, including the Americans With Disabilities Act.
- A requirements section—a list of the education, certifications, licenses, and experience necessary to do the job.

- A section for other important information about the position, such as location, working hours, travel requirements, reporting relationships, and so on.

The Benefits of Using Job Descriptions

Many people consider writing a job description only when it's time to create a new position—and, of course, having a job description will make the task of finding, interviewing, and hiring the right person much easier. However, job descriptions serve a number of other important purposes as well. Job descriptions communicate your expectations and let employees know what it takes to excel in their jobs. Done properly, descriptions can:

- improve employee morale
- enhance communication between you and your employees
- measure future performance
- set the stage to discipline or terminate employees who can't (or won't) meet your expectations, fairly and legally
- improve your ability to retain stellar employees, and
- help you plan for the future.

Why You Need to Know the Law

Many managers are anxious when asked to create job descriptions, because they are afraid they might inadvertently include something that could be used against the company later in a lawsuit. Unfortunately, these fears are not entirely unreasonable: Writing the wrong things in a job description could create major legal problems for your company—and damage to your career.

The good news is that these costly mistakes are entirely avoidable. Done properly, job descriptions can even help prevent lawsuits by laying the groundwork for legal and effective performance evaluation, discipline, and termination. This book gives you all the legal information and practical examples you need to create effective job descriptions that will keep your company on the right side of the law.

Who Should Read This Book

This book is for anyone who has to write or revise a job description—which means anyone who manages employees, from business owners to frontline supervisors. If employees report to you or you are responsible for any aspect of employee relations, you can use this book to create the job descriptions you need to communicate your expectations to employees.

This book is primarily for private sector companies. If you work for the federal, state, or local government, you may have to follow prescribed guidelines for writing job descriptions—or you may be required to keep using descriptions that have been in place for years. Even in this situation, you will still find much of this book useful—you might even be able to convince higher-ups to change their procedures and start writing more effective descriptions, using the techniques in this book!

Different Rules May Apply to Companies With Unions

If employees in your company belong to one or more unions, you may have to use a process for writing and revising job descriptions that differs from the one presented in this book. In a union workplace, the collective bargaining agreement—the contract between the union and the company that defines the rights and obligations of each—may affect how and when you create job descriptions. For example, you may need to get union approval or seek union comment before changing job descriptions, or you may be required to update job descriptions according to a written schedule. Additional complexities might arise if, for instance, you change a job description in a way that takes an employee out of the bargaining unit or makes a position ineligible for certain rights under the collective bargaining agreement. Because of these types of complications, you should talk to a lawyer to find out exactly what's allowed (and what isn't). Do not rely on this book to interpret your collective bargaining agreement.

Who Wrote This Book

Author Margie Mader-Clark has been in the highest levels of the HR profession for more than 15 years, primarily in the fast-paced world of the Silicon Valley. She has experienced firsthand the power of good management—and sadly, the potentially devastating impact of poor management. She practices a simple, commonsense approach in her work in human resources, and this book does the same. Time and again, employees leave companies because of unclear expectations, unfulfilled career opportunities, or lack of advancement. A good hire is the best foundation for a long and positive employment relationship, but clear communication and performance management also play an important role. And the basis of good hiring and managing is communicating exactly what the position entails, starting with the job description. Mader-Clark has implemented and taught these basic principles in companies like Netscape, Hyperion Solutions, and a number of Internet start-ups.

How to Use This Book

This book provides everything you need to create legal and effective job descriptions. In the chapters that follow, you'll find:

- Some job description basics, including the advantages of using them, the many ways in which they can help you in your job as a manager, and an outline of the drafting process. (See Chapter 1.)
- Information that will help you stay on the right side of the law, by avoiding potential legal traps such as disability discrimination issues, contract claims, and problems with overtime classification. (See Chapter 2.)
- Tips and exercises that will help you gather the information you need to write the job description through brainstorming, research, consultation with others, and more. (See Chapter 3.)
- Step-by-step instructions on turning your notes and ideas into a well-crafted, compelling job description. (See Chapter 4.)
- Strategies for using job descriptions in hiring, orientation, performance management, and more. (See Chapter 5.)
- Help with issues that might arise after you finish your description, such as how to handle coworker concerns about the new position and how to accommodate applicants with disabilities. (See Chapter 6.)

The best way to use this book will depend on your goals and experience level. If you are a new manager or are writing your first job description, make the time to read this book from cover to cover. The information you find in each chapter will enable you to write solid descriptions on your first try. In fact, you may want to work on writing an actual job description while reading the book, so you can put the tools and exercises to work in real time!

If you are an old hand at writing job descriptions, but you do so primarily to hire people, spend some time in Chapter Two (on legal traps) and Chapter Five (on using the job description). You will soon see that the job description can be the basis of a healthy work relationship between you and your employees.

If your job responsibilities include training other managers, you'll find the training presentation on the CD-ROM especially helpful. This PowerPoint tool will help you teach a large group of people how to write job descriptions. The presentation can be edited to meet almost any time frame. It follows the book closely, and will enable you to give solid foundational training throughout your organization.

The CD also includes templates for job descriptions, job postings, first-day orientation work plans, and performance management tracking. Additionally, worksheets for exercises in the book are included on the CD, ensuring that you can put these practical tips and tools to use in your everyday work life. (You can also find these documents in Appendix B, and some sample job descriptions in Appendix C.)

Icons Used in This Book

 This icon alerts you to a practical tip or good idea.

 This icon is a caution to consider potential problems you may encounter.

 This icon lets you know that it's time to do a practical exercise that will help you develop your job description.

 If you see this icon, there's a form in Appendix B (and on the CD-ROM at the back of the book) that will help you with the task at hand.

 This icon refers you to related information outside of this book, in other Nolo books or additional resources. ■

Chapter 1

An Overview of Job Descriptions

I f you are like many managers, you probably don't enjoy spending time on job descriptions. You might not know how or where to begin the writing process, or you may simply have too many pressing issues on your plate to justify taking time out to create personnel documents.

But a job description isn't just a piece of paper that sits in an employee's file—it's a living document that will help you hire, manage, encourage, review, and, if necessary, discipline or terminate employees. By clearly stating what you expect of your employees, it provides a solid foundation for all of your management actions.

This chapter provides an overview of the process of creating and using job descriptions. It explains the many advantages of using job descriptions, introduces the ways they can (and should) be used in every stage of the employment relationship, and talks about your role—and the role of others—in the process of creating a job description.

A. Advantages of Creating and Using Job Descriptions

In some companies, job descriptions are dry, outdated documents whose main purpose seems to be taking up space in a filing cabinet. But these companies are missing a tremendous opportunity to improve productivity and morale—and running a high risk of legal trouble in the future.

A well-thought-out job description provides you and the employees who report to you with a blueprint for success. It's the basic tool you use to hire, measure, and manage the performance of each of your employees, and of your team as a whole.

Taking the time to create and update accurate job descriptions will help you in almost every role you play as a manager:

- **The job description is the basis of your search for a new hire.** By clearly defining the job up front in writing, and using that document to make sure candidates know what the job entails, you will have already established and communicated the requirements for success. The job description will also weed out those who don't have the qualifications necessary to do the job, which will save you time in the long run.

- **You can use the job description as an interview tool to help you find the best person for the position.** Once you have the job outlined, you can build your set of interview questions around the job's actual requirements—which will not only help you find a great hire, but also help you steer clear of topics that could lead to legal trouble, such as an applicant's disabilities or private life. And when it's time to choose from your pool of applicants, you will already know exactly what qualities and skills the successful candidate should have.

- **New (or recently promoted) employees can use the job description to get an immediate understanding of what you and the company expect.** By explaining what the job requires up front, before an applicant accepts the job, you can eliminate much of the fear, uncertainty, and doubt that often accompanies the decision to accept a new job. You can also help employees hit the ground running on their very first day of work.

- **The job description is the basis for solid performance management.** Once your employee is on board, you can use the very same job description you used in the hiring process to explain what constitutes success in the job. You can measure how an employee is doing against those expectations, and can help an employee get back on track, if necessary, simply by referring back to the job description. Keeping the description up to date as the position changes will help you coach your employees—and give you standards by which to measure performance fairly and accurately as positions and responsibilities change.

- **Job descriptions are often used to determine pay levels.** By accurately describing what a job entails, and the skills, credentials, and other qualifications necessary to get it done, a job description gives your human resources department a solid way to measure the value of a job and set the pay accordingly. If your company doesn't have a human resources function or a formal compensation program, the description will give you a way to compare this job to other positions in the company when you or others set pay rates—or lobby higher management to budget more money to your department's salaries!

- **Job descriptions can help you limit your company's legal exposure.** If you clearly understand what you are looking for in a position and focus solely on those criteria when filling the job, you will be much less likely to base your hiring decisions on factors that aren't job-related. Your interview questions will be relevant only to the job, and your hiring choices (and performance management decisions) will be based on the person's qualifications and ability to do the job—not on his or her personal characteristics or beliefs, and not on your personal likes or dislikes. This is critical in maintaining a bias-free workplace where employees are treated fairly and consistently. (Discrimination and other legal issues are covered in detail in Chapter 2.)

B. How Job Descriptions Fit Into the Broader Employment Picture

A well-written and frequently updated job description will be useful throughout an employee's tenure with your company, and throughout the "life" of that job. It will serve as:

- a hiring document
- a tool for measuring and managing performance
- a basis for both disciplinary action and celebration of accomplishments
- a basic organizational system to make sure that employees and managers are on the same page with regard to expectations, and
- an important part of your company's legal defense if a former employee files a discrimination or wrongful termination claim.

Although each one of these steps may not occur for every job in every company, you can see that the basic tool used in each of these steps is the job description. (You can find detailed information on how to use job descriptions in each of these situations in Chapter 5.)

1. Defining and Documenting a Position

When you write a job description, you are defining and documenting a position. This process gives you, the manager, an opportunity to clearly describe what you are looking for, including the skills and abilities that will make your team stronger in the future. Being clear and reasonable when you first describe the job will save you a lot of time and trouble in the long run. You will clearly set the expectations for the hire, for the person's performance throughout his or her tenure in the job, and for others who may be interested in that job in the long term.

You also have a great opportunity at this point to think carefully about the current state of your team, their collective skill sets, and what you believe may be necessary to be successful in the future. If you think your team is lacking in certain areas, you can try to bridge the gap by writing a job description that includes those critical skills and functions. If you don't have much input into the directions your company might take in the future, you can use what you know about the company's plans to position your team for success.

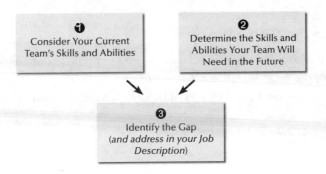

This simple model (commonly known as a "gap analysis") allows you to plan for the future even while you are making sure that the company's present needs are met. Of course, the essential functions of some jobs won't change, even if your company or department does. For example, an accounts payable clerk will most likely always be responsible for assuring that customers pay their invoices in a timely way. Even if your company decides to dump one product line and move into another, the clerk's day-to-day responsibilities will be largely the same. However, if your company is planning to change from one accounting software program to another, then you might want to write a job description that requires expertise in the new program. If you are clever in your hiring, you may even be able to avoid paying for extensive training on the new program. By focusing on the future, you can help your department transition rapidly to the new program and save precious expense dollars along the way.

Managers know all too well that opportunities to plan ahead and set their teams up for success don't present themselves every day. That's why you should take advantage of the job description process to do a little long-range planning whenever possible.

2. Beginning the Hiring Process

When it's time to fill the position, you can use your job description as a tool in planning for the interview. If you formulate your questions directly from the requirements and qualifications listed in the job description, you can make sure that:

- your questions help you identify the best candidate
- your questions don't stray into legally dangerous areas such as marital status, religious beliefs, or other potentially discriminatory issues, and
- you pose similar questions to every applicant for the position, which will allow you to compare their skills and abilities directly—and protect your company from potential discrimination claims.

However, this doesn't mean you have to adhere rigidly to the qualifications described in the description when interviewing, or that you have to ask every applicant exactly the same questions. Instead, you should use the description as a starting point to come up with questions that encourage candidates to talk about their experiences. And when you're actually conducting an interview, don't miss opportunities to ask follow-up questions that delve more deeply into areas the applicant brings up.

EXAMPLE: Your job description for an Animal Trainer reads: "Must be able to apply the principles of Pavlov's theories of behavior to the training of animals." When interviewing applicants, you could simply ask, "Are you able to apply Pavlov's theory of behavior to the training of animals?" The problem is that all but the most dim-witted interview subjects will answer in the affirmative, having figured out that you view this as an important job qualification. And while you've learned something about the candidate's interview skills, you haven't learned much about his or her animal training skills.

If you had instead asked "Have you used Pavlov's theory of behavior in your past training experiences?" and followed up a positive response with questions about how the applicant did so, the answers will be much more informative. You'll learn whether the applicant has actually used the training method, whether he or she understands how the method works, whether the applicant was able to apply it successfully, and what he or she thinks of the method. Instead of asking for a simple yes or no answer, you'll have started a conversation that should yield plenty of information about the candidate's qualifications and skills.

For more information on using job descriptions to plan interviews, see Chapter 5, Section C.

3. Orienting the Employee

Once you've hired someone to fill the position, the job description will let the employee know what to expect. Think back on some of your first days at new jobs. They were most likely filled with doubt, uncertainty, and a little bit of fear. Will I be able to do this job? Will I get along with my coworkers? How long do we get to take for lunch? And where's the bathroom?

Hopefully, you didn't have to wait too long to learn the answers to most of these questions. But imagine how much smoother the process would have been if you were immediately handed a detailed job description for your position, outlining the company's expectations, your responsibilities, your reporting relationships, and more.

By writing well-crafted job descriptions, you can tell your new hires exactly what you expect of them. Employees can sit down with you on their first day of work, prioritize their tasks, figure out what to focus on immediately, and hit the ground running. By helping your new employees become productive more quickly, you'll also save some of the time you would have spent on coaching and training—which will allow you to stay focused on your own job responsibilities.

For more information on using job descriptions for orientation, see Chapter 5, Section D.

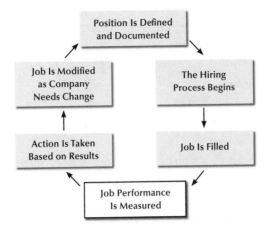

4. Measuring Job Performance

A clear job description sets the stage for good performance by letting employees know what you and the company expect of them. When it's time to do performance evaluations, you can use the job functions spelled out in the job description to measure how employees are doing.

Descriptions also help eliminate arguments about ratings and appraisals: Because a good job description tells employees exactly what they are expected to accomplish, employees won't be able to argue later that you surprised them by using unexpected factors to measure their performance. And because every employee in the same position will be rated on the same performance factors, it will be more difficult for an employee to claim that you were unfairly harsh or imposed additional requirements on him or her—an argument that can form the basis for a discrimination lawsuit.

Turning a job description into a performance evaluation tool is very easy: You simply rate the employee on the job functions listed in the description. (Of course, a complete performance evaluation will probably include other factors, such as ability to work with others, professionalism, and so on.)

EXAMPLE: Here is a section of a job description for a staffing manager. The bullets represent the basic functions of the job.

- Implement the staffing plan, developing high-quality staffing processes and tools in order to:
  - Build Company X's brand as a place to work.
  - Create and implement selection strategies that lead to sustainable, high-performing teams.
  - Build upon Company X's diversity and inclusion programs to assure that the candidate selection pool is populated with people of many and varied viewpoints.
  - Develop robust sourcing strategy that ensures strong candidate flow for Company X's current and future vacancies, and rationalizes costs incurred in the creative use of external search providers.
  - Manage staffing vendor contact negotiations.
  - Recruit executive-level candidates.
  - Create and implement College Recruiting Program.

Turning this description into a measurement tool is as easy as adding a rating section. In this example, you can use a simple numerical scale, ranging from a "1" for very poor performance to a "5" for outstanding performance.

TASK	RATING
• Build Company X's brand as a place to work.	
• Create and implement selection strategies that lead to sustainable, high-performing teams.	
• Build upon Company X's diversity and inclusion programs to assure that the candidate selection pool is populated with people of many and varied viewpoints.	
• Develop robust sourcing strategy that ensures strong candidate flow for Company X's current and future vacancies, and rationalizes costs incurred in the creative use of external search providers.	
• Manage staffing vendor contract negotiations.	
• Recruit executive-level candidates.	
• Create and implement College Recruiting Program.	

Using this simple worksheet taken straight from the job description, you can rate your employee's performance quickly, gather feedback on the employee from coworkers and others, and share the results with the employee. See Chapter 5, Section E, for tips that will help you use job descriptions to measure performance.

Need help with performance evaluations? *The Performance Appraisal Handbook,* by Amy DelPo (Nolo), provides a step-by-step system for measuring employee performance—and communicating that information effectively.

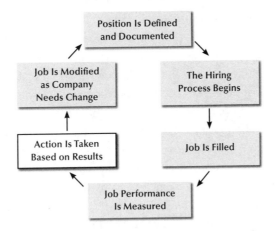

5. Taking Action Based on the Job Description

For employees who are either exceeding your expectations or struggling to improve, you can use the job description as a benchmark for how things "should" be going. Let's take poor performance first. If an employee is falling short in specific areas, you can refer to the job description when you meet with the employee to discuss the problem. Whether you are raising the issue in a casual conversation or following your company's formal disciplinary procedures, using the job description will give you a point of reference for your conversation—and remind you to limit your comments to the employee's performance issues, not personal traits or characteristics.

Many companies follow a progressive discipline policy, by which managers first bring problems to the employee's attention through a verbal warning, then one or more written warnings, then suspension or termination if the employee is unable or unwilling to improve. You can use the job description at every point in this type of process.

1. **Verbal warning:** Refer to the job description to highlight areas of concern and, if necessary, help your employee understand what is going wrong. Relying on the requirements set out in the description, come up with a plan to improve the problem.

2. **Written reprimand (often referred to as a Performance Plan or Performance Improvement Plan (PIP)):** If the problem continues, you can issue a written warning and hold a more detailed counseling session. Use the job description to come up with a written action plan that requires the employee to show improvement towards meeting the job requirements in a measured time frame.

3. **Suspension or termination:** If you have put together a fair action plan, and provided both reasonable time for improvement and any resources necessary for success, an employee who still doesn't meet your requirements has shown an inability or unwillingness to do the job. Because you have used your job description at every stage of employment, from hiring to orientation to evaluating performance to discipline, you can show that the employee knew all along what you and the company expected—and that the employee failed to meet those requirements. This will make it very tough for the employee to argue that he or she was wrongfully terminated.

Strong performance can also be measured by the original job description. If your employee is really hitting the ball out of the park, schedule a meeting to let him or her know how thrilled you are! You can use the job description to show exactly how great a job the employee is doing.

This is also an ideal opportunity to discuss the possibility of assigning new responsibilities to the employee. There may be some logical additions to the employee's current workload, or you may brainstorm together to come up with ways to keep things interesting and challenging. Remember, if you decide together to alter the job, you should update the job description to make sure it accurately reflects what you both believe the job to be.

For more information on using job descriptions to manage performance, see Chapter 5, Section E.

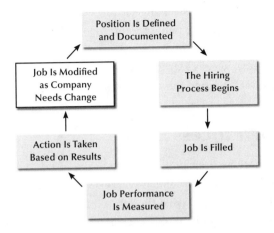

6. Modifying a Job Based on Company Needs

As you work to keep up with the changing demands of the company, you should update the job descriptions of positions that report to you to reflect new developments and needs.

> **EXAMPLE:** John manages an auto body shop specializing in Toyonda sport-utility vehicles. All of his mechanics are certified by Toyonda, have a minimum of seven years of experience in repairing these vehicles, and are equally familiar with every SUV Toyonda makes.
>
> John receives a letter from Toyonda America announcing the arrival of the Toyonda Hybrid SUV—a modern ecological marvel with a new type of engine that uses both gas and electricity. John is quick to realize that his mechanics' jobs are about to change. He needs to make sure that his shop can handle repairs to these new vehicles.
>
> John pulls out his trusty Mechanic I Job Description. He adds a bullet to the job functions section, stating that mechanics must be certified in hybrid SUV repair. With this new description in hand, he meets with his mechanics to talk about how they can meet the new requirement—for example, John might offer to pay for a training session. Or, John could hire a new mechanic who is already familiar with the hybrid, and let him or her handle all repairs on the new vehicles.
>
> John has responded to the changing conditions of his workforce in a simple, effective way—and it all started with updating a job description.

As the needs of your business change, you need to respond by keeping your workforce up to date on the changing requirements. Changing the job description is an easy way to track and communicate these developments—and make sure you have the resources necessary to succeed in the new regime.

For information on updating job descriptions, see Chapter 6, Sections C and D.

C. The Drafting Process

Of course, the primary responsibility for writing the job description falls on you. You will manage the position for which you are writing the description, so you have some unique insights into what the job requires.

This doesn't mean that you should write the job description in a vacuum, however. In fact, getting others in the company—from your boss to other managers to any employees who will report to the position—involved in the process will make your job description more accurate and complete.

1. Your Role

You will have four basic responsibilities in putting together the job description:

1. **Write the first draft.** Even if you don't know every single thing about the position, you can certainly take the first stab at describing it. The information and exercises in Chapter 3 will help you gather and analyze the information you need. And the tips and examples in Chapter 4 will help you turn your ideas into a compelling and accurate description.

2. **Gather input from others.** Once you have completed a draft, you should circulate it to others and ask them for their comments. (See Section 2, below, for information on who should be involved.) This input will make the job description as accurate and relevant as possible—and help you make sure that you didn't leave out anything important.

3. **Incorporate the input from others.** Once you gather feedback from others, you should revise the job description to include all relevant input. You'll have to be selective, however—if your boss gives you a long "wish list" of qualities the ideal candidate should have, for example, you may have to pare it down to the essentials.

4. **Update as necessary.** Once the description is complete, don't just throw it in a drawer and forget about it. A job description is a living document that may need to be revised as the job requirements change. In fact, you may meet

an ideal candidate who can actually do more or different things than you originally outlined, which means you may have to update the job description before you even make a hire! As your team and your company change, make sure your job descriptions remain up to date. And remember to share any changes you make with the person actually doing the job, to keep everybody on the same page.

2. The Role of Others

Who else should you involve when you create a job description? Consider a standard organizational chart:

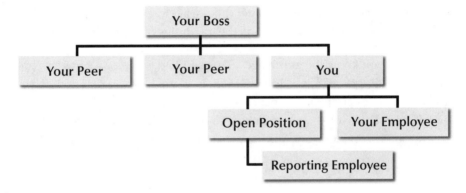

If this chart were to reflect how your open position will interact with others in your group or company, it might look something like this:

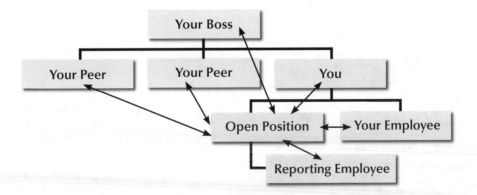

With all these people relying on this position in some way, doesn't it make sense to gather their input on what the job requires? Each will bring a unique perspective to the overall job description that you may not be able to come up with on your own. The end result will be a well-rounded job that answers the needs of all those that will eventually work with this position.

Keep it simple. The more people who provide feedback on the job's requirements, the harder you will have to work to keep the job description reasonable. Although many people may have valuable input and ideas, it is ultimately your job to draft a description that is straightforward and achievable. If you discover that too many people have too many expectations of the person who will fill the job, it might be time to consider other ways to get this work done, like hiring more than one person or shuffling the job duties of your existing reports.

Now that you know the advantages of using job descriptions, how they are used in the life cycle of a job, and your role in writing the job description, you are probably eager to put pencil to paper (or fingers to keyboard) and start writing. But before you do, you'll need to know the potential legal pitfalls associated with writing job descriptions—and how to avoid them. These are covered in Chapter 2.

Test Your Knowledge

Questions

1. You don't have to write your own job descriptions—you can just download a standard template from the Internet.   ❐ True   ❐ False

2. It is easy to hire a well-qualified person even without a job description.   ❐ True   ❐ False

3. You can use the job description to craft good interview questions.   ❐ True   ❐ False

4. A well-written job description can give the person already doing the job a good roadmap for being successful.   ❐ True   ❐ False

5. Proper use of a job description in the interview process is a foolproof way to keep out of court.   ❐ True   ❐ False

6. Job descriptions should be used primarily during the hiring process.   ❐ True   ❐ False

7. It is important to note on a job description whether you prefer a man or a woman for the position.   ❐ True   ❐ False

8. As long as an employee is performing well, you won't need to refer to the job description to manage him or her.   ❐ True   ❐ False

9. If you use the job description to measure employee performance, you are in danger of confusing your employee.   ❐ True   ❐ False

10. As the person who will manage the position, you are the sole source of information in creating the job description.   ❐ True   ❐ False

Answers

1. **False.** A job description won't be effective unless it accurately describes the position and its requirements. No form you download from the Web can do this for you.

2. **False.** It is more difficult to make a quality hire without understanding everything the position requires—and whether your applicant can meet those requirements.

3. **True.** Because the job description includes the essential functions of the position, you can use it as a basis for an interview that effectively explores whether applicants can do the job.

4. **True.** You can always measure a person's success against your original expectations, as laid out in the job description.

5. **False.** While job descriptions are very helpful, there is no "foolproof" way to stay out of court.

6. **False.** You will find the job description an excellent tool throughout the life cycle of a job, from hiring to managing to refilling or restructuring a position.

7. **False.** Your job description should focus solely on the job and its real requirements. Including preferences like these can lead to discrimination lawsuits—and prevent you from reaching the broadest possible applicant pool.

8. **False.** The job description can help you determine just how much your star employee is exceeding the original requirements of the job. It can also help you decide whether to add or change the duties of the job to keep it challenging and fulfilling.

9. **False.** The job description tells employees exactly what your company expects, and should be the basis for measuring their performance.

10. **False.** The more input you have from others who may interact with the job, the richer and more accurate the job description will be. ■

Chapter 2

Avoiding Legal Pitfalls

Many of you will embark on this chapter with a sense of anxiety. You have probably heard horror stories about employment lawsuits, how they can sink good companies and ruin the careers of well-meaning people. Although you may have heard some exaggerated tales, the sad truth is that many of your most basic managerial tasks—and many of the decisions you have to make every day at work—could lead your company into legal trouble, if you're not careful.

But don't despair. There is good news, too: Employment law, as it relates to writing job descriptions, is not that complicated—and it's based primarily on common sense. This chapter will give you all of the information you need to make sure the job descriptions you write won't put your company at legal risk.

You don't need an entire reference book on employment law to write a legally sound job description. In fact, all you really need to do is follow these basic rules, each of which is described more fully below:

- Don't discriminate. (See Section A, below.)
- Don't undermine at-will employment. (See Section B, below.)
- Don't make promises you can't keep. (See Section C, below.)
- Don't violate applicants' privacy. (See Section D, below.)
- Don't create overtime classification problems. (See Section E, below.)

A. Don't Discriminate

Perhaps the most common—and most costly—mistake managers make when writing job descriptions is to include language that could be interpreted as discriminatory. Federal and state laws prohibit discrimination in every phase of the employment relationship, which includes writing job descriptions and using them for hiring, evaluating performance, discipline, and so on.

Federal law prohibits discrimination on the basis of race, national origin, religion, sex (including pregnancy), citizenship status, age (for employees who are at least 40), and disability. Legally, these categories are called "protected characteristics," because employees are protected from discrimination on the basis of these traits.

These laws don't apply to every company, however. Most federal antidiscrimination laws—which include Title VII of the Civil Rights Act, the Age Discrimination in Employment Act (ADEA), the Equal Pay Act, the Immigration Reform and Control Act, and the Americans with Disabilities Act—apply only to companies with a certain minimum number of employees. (See "Which Federal Antidiscrimination Laws Apply to Your Company," below, for more information.) However, many state laws apply more broadly—they may apply to smaller employers and may include additional protected characteristics, such as marital status or sexual orientation. (See the chart, "State Laws Prohibiting Discrimination in Employment," in Appendix D, for more information. Appendix D also includes contact information for state agencies that enforce discrimination laws.)

Which Federal Antidiscrimination Laws Apply to Your Company

Not every antidiscrimination law applies to every employer. Federal antidiscrimination laws apply only to employers with more than a minimum number of employees—and this minimum number is different for each law.

NAME OF LAW:	DISCRIMINATION PROHIBITED ON THE BASIS OF:	APPLIES TO:
Title VII	Race, national origin, religion, sex	Employers with 15 or more employees
Age Discrimination in Employment Act	Age (against employees age 40 and over only)	Employers with 20 or more employees
Americans with Disabilities Act	Physical or mental disability	Employers with 15 or more employees
Equal Pay Act	Sex (applies only to wage discrimination)	All Employers
Immigration Reform and Control Act	Citizenship status, national origin	Employers with 4 or more employees

1. General Rules to Avoid Discrimination

Before you can understand how to avoid discriminating, you have to know what discrimination is. In legal terms, a manager discriminates by treating an applicant or employee differently because of his or her protected characteristic (race, gender, and so on). For example, it is discrimination to refuse to hire an older applicant because of his or her age; to refuse to promote any women to higher management positions; or to use stricter standards when evaluating the performance of African-American or Latino employees.

When Protected Characteristics Are Essential to the Job

There are very limited circumstances when the law recognizes that certain jobs call for certain types of people. For example, you will need to hire a Catholic if you are looking for a priest of a Catholic church, and you probably won't want to hire any men to be attendants in your company ladies' room. In these situations, the law creates a very limited exception to the federal antidiscrimination laws, which allows you to base your employment decisions on a protected characteristic (except for race, which is always off-limits) if the very nature of the job requires it. Legally, the term for this exception is "bona fide occupational qualification," known in shorthand as "BFOQ."

If you are writing a job description for this type of job, you should clearly spell out the BFOQ(s) in your job description. Be warned, however, that there are very few cases in which courts have upheld an employer's claimed BFOQ. If you are challenged by an employee, your company will have to show that the BFOQ is an ironclad necessity for doing the job—that is, that virtually no one who falls outside the protected category could perform the job's functions. Because this is such a tough test to meet, you should talk to a lawyer before deciding to include it in your job description and rely on it in your job decisions.

So how do you avoid these types of discrimination? By focusing solely on the requirements of the job and keeping a careful eye on your language. If you stick to the job's essential functions, you should have no need to specify the race, religion, or other protected characteristics of applicants for the position. Even if your company focuses on a particular demographic group—for example, it creates fitness clothing designed especially for women, manufactures Thai food products, or publishes books about ancient Jewish mysticism—that doesn't mean that your employees must be members of these groups. As long as they have the requisite skills, experience, and qualifications, you may not discriminate against them on this basis.

However, even if you don't specify gender, national origin, or other protected characteristics in the job description, you can still run into trouble if you describe a job function or requirement that disproportionately excludes applicants from certain groups. Under a legal theory called "disparate impact," employers can be sued for discrimination if they adopt an apparently neutral policy that has a disproportionate negative effect on a protected group. For example, if your job description requires all applicants to have a college degree, you may exclude more employees of certain races. Similarly, if your job description includes a strength or lifting requirement, you might exclude a disproportionate number of female applicants.

Of course, these types of requirements may be perfectly legitimate. For example, a person who works loading and unloading heavy packages in a warehouse must have some strength to do the job. The law recognizes this dilemma and allows employers to defend against a disparate impact claim by showing that the requirement in question is job-related and necessary to the business. When you're writing a job description, this means that every requirement and qualification you list should be absolutely necessary to do the job.

Language and Fluency Requirements

Because an applicant's accent and English language skills are often closely associated with his or her national origin, special rules apply to language or fluency requirements: the law recognizes that such requirements may well be perfectly reasonable, but they must be legitimate and necessary.

A company may refuse to hire employees who are not fluent in English only if English language skills are required to effectively perform the position—and this will vary from job to job within a company. For example, employees who staff the customer service or concierge counter at a hotel probably need good communication skills and the ability to speak and understand English; employees who maintain the grounds of the same hotel probably don't.

Similar rules apply to employees or applicants who speak with an accent. An employer may decide not to hire or promote an employee to a position that requires clear oral communication in English if the employee's accent substantially affects his or her ability to communicate clearly. However, if the employee's accent does not impair his or her ability to be understood, an employer may not make job decisions on that basis—for example, a company cannot simply adopt a blanket rule that employees who speak accented English may not work in customer service positions.

Finally, make sure that your language is inclusive. For example, many of the terms used for various jobs are gendered (such as handyman, barmaid, waitress, or salesman). Although it may seem unwieldy, you should always use gender-neutral terms (repairperson or salesperson) in your job descriptions. Also, check to make sure your language doesn't imply a preference for younger workers (the words "energetic," "youthful," "college student," and "recent graduate" should be avoided, for example).

2. Avoiding Disability Discrimination

The Americans with Disabilities Act (42 U.S.C. §§ 12101-12213) prohibits private employers with at least 15 employees from discriminating in any aspect of employment against a person with a disability. The law protects "qualified workers with disabilities" from discrimination—that is, applicants and workers who can do the essential functions of the job, with or without a reasonable accommodation. Your legal obligations when writing and using job descriptions stem from how these terms are defined:

- A qualified worker is one who has the necessary experience, skills, training, licenses, and so on to do the job. If a worker needs a reasonable accommodation for his or her disability in order to perform the job's essential functions, that fact alone doesn't make the worker unqualified.
- A worker with a disability is someone who has a long-term physical or mental impairment that substantially limits a major life activity (such as the ability to walk, talk, see, hear, breathe, reason, work, or take care of oneself). Workers are also protected from discrimination if they have a history of disability (for example, they suffered cancer or depression in the past) or the employer believes, incorrectly, that they have a disability—this sometimes comes up when a worker has an obvious impairment (such as a limp or speech impediment) that is not actually disabling.
- Essential job function are the fundamental duties of the position—those things that the person holding the job absolutely must be able to do.
- Reasonable accommodations are assistance and/or changes to the workplace or job that will enable a worker with a disability to do the job. For example, a worker in a wheelchair might need a lower desktop, or a worker with impaired hearing may need special telephone equipment.

a. Designate Essential Job Functions

To avoid unfairly screening out workers with disabilities, you should carefully distinguish the essential functions of the position in your job description. Some managers and companies include only essential functions in their job descriptions; others list functions that are not essential separately, under a heading such as "Nonessential Functions" or "Additional Responsibilities." Either strategy will work: The key is to make sure that applicants—and those who do the hiring in your company—understand which functions are essential (and which are not).

Distinguishing essential functions will determine your company's legal obligations towards applicants and employees with disabilities. If a function is truly essential, and the applicant or employee cannot do it even with a reasonable accommodation, that person is not considered "qualified" for the job as a legal matter (and you don't have to worry about discrimination lawsuits based on your refusal to hire him or her). If, on the other hand, a function is not essential, an employee's or applicant's inability to do it because of a disability cannot legally play a role in your hiring decision.

It can be tough to figure out which job duties are essential. You are going to need to ask yourself frequently if the functions you are describing are absolutely necessary to doing the job successfully. The Equal Employment Opportunity Commission (EEOC), the federal agency that enforces the ADA and other antidiscrimination laws, looks at these factors in determining whether a function is essential:

- the employer's assessment of which functions are essential, as demonstrated by job descriptions written before the employer posts or advertises for the position

Job descriptions written after the fact can work against you. Courts and the EEOC understand that they don't know all of the ins and outs of your company's business. That's why, in a disability discrimination case, they will give due consideration to your judgment about which functions are essential to the position. A job description prepared before you enlist any candidates is a solid piece of evidence supporting your assessment of essential functions. But a job description prepared after you find out about an applicant's disability (or worse, after that applicant accuses your company of discriminating) looks more like evidence of a cover-up. This is just one more reason to prepare written job descriptions before you need to use them.

- whether the position exists to perform that function
- the experience of workers who actually hold that position

- the time spent performing that function
- the consequences of not performing the function
- whether other employees are available to perform that function, and
- the degree of expertise or skill required to perform the function.

Example: Janine is writing a job description for a grocery store cashier reporting to her. Janine knows that the job includes requirements like basic math skills, good customer service, and knowledge of the products grocery stores carry. She also believes that it is necessary for the cashier to be able to lift decent amounts of weight, as the products purchased sometimes include cases of soda, bags of dog food, and other heavy items. So Janine decides that the ability to lift up to 25 pounds is an essential job function, and includes it in the job description.

She finishes writing her description and forwards it to the store's legal counsel for review. It comes back with the 25-pound lifting requirement removed. Why? In the lawyer's opinion, this requirement is not an essential element of the cashier job. Baggers, whose job duties include not only lifting heavy items into and out of carts, but also helping customers load these items into their cars, are typically available to perform that function, so cashiers rarely have to do it. If Janine had been writing a job description for a bagger, the lifting requirement would probably have stayed in as an essential job function.

You'll have to stand by your designations. Once you describe certain job duties as essential or nonessential, you will have to stick with those classifications. Remember, the purpose of labeling essential functions is to make it easier for you and for disabled applicants to determine whether they are qualified for the position. If your job description classifies a task as nonessential, you could be in legal trouble if you refuse to hire a disabled applicant because he or she cannot perform that task.

b. Describe the Results, Not the Process

To avoid violating the law—and to make sure you don't inadvertently miss out on a great applicant with a disability—you should write a job description that focuses on what the employee must accomplish, not on how the employee has to get it done. That way, applicants who could do the job with some form of reasonable accommodation won't be discouraged or unfairly screened out of the hiring process.

EXAMPLE: Annie is the director of an Internet marketing team whose job is to promote online dating. She has an open position for a marketing manager who will be working with affiliate vendors and managing ad space on the site. She believes that the best way to do business with the company's vendors is to talk with them, frequently and directly. So she puts this requirement on her list of essential functions: Excellent verbal and written communications skills are a must.

Annie writes up her job description, and includes this bullet. Later that night, as she relaxes by watching *West Wing,* she sees a character played by Marlee Matlin, the hearing—impaired actress. The character's disability is accommodated by an interpreter, which has no impact on the quality of work that she provides for the fictional White House. This starts Annie thinking about her position. Could this job be done by someone who has significant problems with verbal communication? If the negotiations with vendors are done by email or written presentation, a person with this type of disability could very well do the job. What Annie is really concerned with is that the marketing manager establishes strong vendor relationships, not how they go about doing so.

If you find these nondiscrimination rules daunting, remember that they stem from a very basic (and imminently sensible) idea: that the employment decisions you make as a manager should be based on legitimate, job-related criteria. As applied to job descriptions, this means you absolutely can consider the qualifications, experience, skills, and so on that are necessary to do the job—and you should not consider factors that are not job-related, such as race, religion, or disability. If you follow this simple rule, you'll keep your company out of legal trouble; you'll also make smarter and more effective managerial decisions.

B. Don't Undermine At-Will Employment

As a manager, you've probably heard the term "employment at will." Unlike many legal terms, employment at will means just about what it sounds like: at-will employees are free to quit at any time, for any reason; and employers are free to fire them at any time and for any reason—unless the reason for firing is illegal (for example, the employee is fired because of his or her race, religion, or other protected characteristic—see Section A, above, for more on discrimination).

Under the laws of every state (except Montana), employment is assumed to be at will. But employers can restrict or give up their right to fire at will by creating an employment contract limiting this right. There may be circumstances when this makes good business sense. For example, if an employer wants to make sure a high-level employee stays on for a year, it might ask the employee to agree not to quit for that period of time, in exchange for the company's promise not to fire the employee during the same period. Although these types of contracts can be made orally, they are typically in writing and signed by both parties.

However, employers can also give up their at-will rights inadvertently, by creating an implied contract—an agreement that is never actually written or stated, but that a court will assume existed, based on the actions, statements, and conduct of the parties. This is what you have to worry about when writing your job descriptions. If you include any language that might lead applicants to believe they will have job security, will be fired only for specified reasons, or will be assured of raises and promotions as long as their work is satisfactory, you risk undermining the right to fire at will. A fired employee could use the job description as one piece of evidence to prove that he or she had an employment contract limiting your company's right to fire for any reason.

Here are some examples of statements that could lead to trouble:

- "Success at Task A will ensure ongoing employment."
- "Position is a stepping-stone for promotion to the next level."
- "Candidates who can meet these challenges have a bright future at our company."
- "Those who successfully complete the company's probation period will become permanent employees."
- "This is a permanent position."

The problem with each of these statements is that they imply—or out-and-out say—that the job will last indefinitely or for a stated period of time, or that the employee will have a job as long as he or she performs well. As long as you focus on simply describing the qualifications and requirements necessary to do the job, rather than making statements about the employee's future at the company, you'll do just fine.

Consider including a disclaimer in your job descriptions. Some companies routinely state, in the description itself, that the job description is not a contract between the employee and the company, and that the company has the right to change the employee's job duties at its discretion. This type of language can help a company prove that it preserved its at-will rights; it can also help defeat an employee's claim that he or she was entitled to the exact job detailed in the description, without change, for the term of his or her employment at the company. Talk to your human resources or legal department to find out whether you should include this type of disclaimer in your job descriptions.

> **SAMPLE DISCLAIMER:** This document describes the position currently available. It is not an employment contract. Our company reserves the right to modify job duties or job descriptions at any time.

C. Don't Make Promises You Can't (or Won't) Keep

In the heat of trying to market your open position and attract that elusive perfect candidate, you may be tempted to exaggerate, overstate, or simply offer more than you (or your company) can deliver. For example, you may be considering saying something like "position offers valuable stock option grants." But what if those stock options aren't so valuable after all, or the employee you hire doesn't work out as you had hoped?

There are two types of legal problems that can arise from making promises in a job description. First, you risk creating a contract between your company and the employee—the unspoken agreement is "If you accept this position, you will receive valuable stock option grants." Once the employee accepts the position, thereby holding up his or her end of the deal, your company will have to come through on its promise or risk a lawsuit for breach of contract.

The second (and closely related) problem is lawsuits for fraud. If an employee can show that you made false statements or promises (that is, you made promises without knowing whether or not they would be fulfilled) and the employee took the job on the basis of your misrepresentations, the employee may be able to sue for fraud or a similar state law claim. After all, the employee may have quit a secure and well-paying job on the basis of your statements, so it's only fair to ask your company to make good.

Avoiding these problems isn't too tough: focus on describing the job, not outright overselling it. Make sure every statement you write accurately describes the position. Don't make any promises unless you know they will be fulfilled. For instance, if you write, "Position will receive annual merit increases," you have made a promise to increase that person's salary every year they work at your company—and that's not a promise you know is going to come true. If you instead wrote, "Position will be eligible for annual merit increases," you have promised only that the new hire will be considered for an annual raise—which is really about the only commitment you can make at this point.

D. Don't Violate Applicants' Privacy

You might be wondering how a job description could violate someone's privacy. After all, a job description is a document, not a surveillance camera or an interrogation technique. But things you include in a job description might encourage whoever uses the description to snoop around where they don't belong.

For example, if your job description includes any reference to candidates' private lives, marital status, political opinions, off-duty conduct, or other areas most of us would consider personal, the person who conducts interviews or performance evaluations for the position using your description might feel compelled to ask about these issues. And applicants will probably believe they have to talk about these issues in order to get the job.

If It's Really a Job Requirement, It's Not a Privacy Violation

You might be wondering about job duties that require employees to bare their souls—or their bodies—but really are essential to the job. For example, what if you're hiring a nude model to pose for art classes? If it's a recognized and essential job requirement, the answer is that you should probably include it in the job description.

That's what the Feminist Women's Health Center (FWHC) did. FWHC hired someone whose job duties included performing cervical self-examinations in front of clients and other employees, as a means of demonstrating the procedure. This job duty was clearly described in the job description, which FWHC attached to its job application and required applicants to read.

One employee refused to do the exams, and was eventually moved to a different position. After she was fired, the employee sued for wrongful termination, claiming that a job requirement that entailed disrobing and exposing herself violated her right of privacy.

The court ruled in favor of the Health Center. Although the court found that the requirement invaded the employee's privacy rights, it also found that it was a reasonable condition of employment, given the Health Center's unique mission and methods of educating women about reproductive health. Most important to the court was the fact that the employee agreed to this job condition, as evidenced by its inclusion in the job description that was appended to the application. *Feminist Women's Health Center v. Superior Court* (Jenkins), 52 Cal.App.4th 1234 (1997).

Similarly, some managers specify selection criteria in a job description that could result in invading the applicant's privacy. Perhaps the most common example is a testing requirement—psychological testing, in particular. Courts have held that psychological tests can invade an applicant's privacy, depending on the questions asked and the way the answers are used in the selection process. If your company requires testing of applicants, you should probably talk to a lawyer.

E. Don't Create Overtime Classification Problems

To reap the benefits of using job descriptions, you have to describe the job's actual functions and requirements—but you don't want to inadvertently throw in any terms that a court might interpret differently than your company does, particularly when it comes to determining whether the position is eligible for overtime. Typically, this problem comes up when a company seeks to defend its position that a particular employee was not entitled to earn overtime, but the job description undermines its argument. Courts and government agencies ultimately decide this issue based on the employee's actual job duties, not on job descriptions or other documents, but it's best to avoid inconsistencies that you'll have to explain later.

There are very specific rules that determine whether a particular employee is entitled to earn overtime—time-and-a-half for every hour worked over 40 a week under federal law. Some states have different overtime standards or even daily overtime requirements. Employers are obligated to follow whichever laws, state or federal, offer their employees more protection, so you'll want to know your state's rules. Contact your state labor department for more information (contact information is in Appendix D).

An employee's entitlement to overtime is based on his or her job duties and compensation. Any employee who earns less than $455 per week ($23,660 per year) is automatically entitled to overtime, as long as the employer is covered by the Fair Labor Standards Act, the federal law that governs wages and hours (and most are). Employees who earn more than this threshold are entitled to overtime if they are engaged in certain professions—manual laborers and first responders are two positions that are entitled to overtime regardless of how much they are paid, for example.

Beyond these rules, however, it gets a little more complicated. Generally, employees whose work requires a fair degree of independent thinking and discretion, high-level decision making, management responsibility, advanced study, or creativity are less likely to be entitled to overtime than those who perform fairly routine clerical or line work. Here is a brief overview of the most common categories of exempt employees (an employee who is not entitled to earn overtime is referred to as "exempt"; an employee who is entitled to overtime is referred to as "nonexempt"):

- **Executive:** The position's primary duty is to manage an enterprise, department, or subdepartment of the company. The position must manage at least two employees and have the ability to hire or fire (or have significant input into these decisions). Managers, directors, and executive officers often fall into this exemption category.

- **Administrative:** The position's primary duty is to perform office or other nonmanual work directly related to the management or general business operations of the company. The position must also require the exercise of discretion or independent judgment. An assistant to the company's chief executive officer might fall into this category.

- **Learned professional:** The position's primary duty is work requiring advanced intellectual knowledge in the fields of science or learning. This advanced knowledge must be acquired by a prolonged course of specialized intellectual instruction. Lawyers, doctors, and scientists typically find themselves in this category.

- **Creative professional:** This position's primary duty is performing work that requires invention, imagination, originality, or talent in a recognized field of artistic or creative endeavor. Examples include movie directors or actors, writers, and graphic designers.

- **Certain computer specialists:** This category includes computer systems analysts, computer programmers, software engineers, or other similarly skilled workers in the computer field.

Get more information on federal overtime rules. You'll find lots of information, including factsheets, answers to common questions, and more, at the website of the Department of Labor, at www.dol.gov. From the home page, click "Overtime Security" to get to the department's overtime resources.

Now that you know a little bit about the most common exemption categories, you can probably see how easy it could be to create confusion—especially if you are trying to make a job sound fancier than it really is.

EXAMPLE 1: John is a manager at a large financial institution. He needs to hire a secretary to do routine paperwork and answer phones. John sits down to write his job description. First, he decides to call this an "executive assistant" position, to make it sound more important. Next, he lists as an essential function, "Position requires independent thinking and ability to use good judgment in making significant decisions." John is referring to the secretary's ability to screen calls and decide which clients must be put through immediately, but it sure sounds like he is describing a high-level administrator under the overtime rules. If the company decides, based on John's job description, not to pay the secretary overtime, it could end up on the wrong end of a wage and hour lawsuit. This is not the type of position that is typically exempt from overtime.

EXAMPLE 2: Now consider the opposite problem. Jack is hiring a manager for his bookstore. The manager will be responsible for hiring and supervising ten employees, cashing out the registers and making bank deposits, deciding which books to order for the store, choosing store displays, planning author readings and other events, stocking shelves, answering customer questions, and much more. In his job description, Jack lists the essential functions briefly, as "Manager must be able to work well with others, be aware of current trends in the book business, and have ability to juggle many responsibilities at once. Duties will include stocking books, assisting customers, promoting special events, and other responsibilities as necessary." Although Jack's bookstore manager is probably not entitled to earn overtime, you wouldn't know that from the job description, which doesn't detail any of the important responsibilities of the position. If Jack's manager decides to press the issue, this job description won't help Jack at all.

So how do you avoid overtime classification problems? By being accurate in your job descriptions, and by avoiding buzzwords like "independent judgment," "discretion," "exempt," "nonexempt," and so on. This will give others in your company the information they need to correctly classify the position—and will avoid giving unhappy employees ammunition to attack your company's overtime policies. If your company includes overtime classifications on its descriptions (some include a check box for "exempt" or "nonexempt," for example), let your legal or human resources department make this decision.

Equal Pay Considerations

Classification problems can also come up under the Equal Pay Act (EPA), although this is less common. Under the EPA, men and women are entitled to equal pay for equal work. As long as two positions have different responsibilities or requirements, or require different types of skills or effort, it's perfectly legal to pay male and female employees at different rates for doing them. But if the positions are the same, men and women must be paid at the same rate for doing them—even if they have different names. For example, even if female cleaning staff in a hotel are called "maids" and male cleaning staff are called "housekeeping technicians," they are entitled to equal pay if they are doing the same work.

This is another problem that can be avoided with accurate job descriptions. If two positions really are different, the job descriptions should be different as well. This will help you prove, if you need to, that the jobs really are dissimilar. On the other hand, if you use the same job description to hire for positions that are actually different, you could be asking for legal trouble.

Test Your Knowledge

Questions

1. Title VII of the Civil Rights Act of 1964 protects gay men and lesbians from employment discrimination based on their sexual orientation. ❏ True ❏ False

2. Under the Equal Pay Act, workers must receive equal pay for equal work regardless of their age. ❏ True ❏ False

3. In crafting your job description, you shouldn't make any statement that promises continued employment. ❏ True ❏ False

4. If your company usually gives annual raises, you should put that in your job description. ❏ True ❏ False

5. Under the ADA, it is your duty to provide a reasonable accommodation to employees or applicants with disabilities. ❏ True ❏ False

6. If a disabled applicant cannot perform the job's essential functions, even with a reasonable accommodation, that applicant is not qualified for the job and you don't have to hire him or her. ❏ True ❏ False

7. In the State of Wisconsin, it is illegal to discriminate against those with Military Service or Status.
(Hint: Check the chart in Appendix D!) ❏ True ❏ False

8. A well-written job description is an easy way to run afoul of Federal employment law. ❏ True ❏ False

Answers

1. **False.** Title VII protects against discrimination based on race or color, religion, sex, pregnancy, childbirth, and national origin. However, some states do prohibit discrimination based on sexual orientation—see "State Laws Prohibiting Discrimination in Employment," in Appendix D.

2. **False.** The Equal Pay Act requires that employers pay men and women equal wages for doing equal work.

3. **True.** Promising continued employment could be seen as an implied contract—and could tie your company's hands in future dealings with that employee.

4. **False.** This would be construed as a written contract and would necessitate paying a raise even if the rest of the company is not receiving one, or if the employee did not earn one. It is a promise that you may not be able to keep.

5. **True.** If a disabled employee needs a reasonable accommodation to do the job, you must provide it unless it would pose an undue hardship.

6. **True.** An employee who cannot do a job's essential functions, with or without a reasonable accommodation, is not qualified for the job.

7. **True.** Familiarize yourself with your own state laws using the chart "State Laws Prohibiting Discrimination in Employment," in Appendix D.

8. **False.** A well-written job description is actually a great way to stay out of legal trouble. By focusing it on the responsibilities and qualifications of the job, you are protecting yourself and your company against discrimination claims. And, because you can use the job description to let employees know what you expect, it also lays the groundwork for documented discipline and, if necessary, termination for employees who can't do the job. ∎

Chapter 3

Analyze and Define the Job

To create or update a job description, you can't simply sit down and start writing. Before you begin your first draft, you'll need to have a good sense of the requirements and duties of the position—and of how that position will fit within your team and your company, both now and in the future. That means you have to start by gathering information. By spending some time analyzing and defining the job up front, you will be able to craft an accurate, complete, and legally sound description that will stand the test of time.

As explained in the Introduction, a job description has four basic parts:

- a summary of the position
- a list of job functions (that is, what the person holding this job will actually do on a day-to-day basis)
- the qualifications necessary to do the job, and
- any other job requirements (such as travel or odd work hours).

This chapter will help you gather the information you need to complete each of these sections. It explains how to:

- Consider the big picture: What's happening in the current business and economic environment, and what changes do you anticipate for your team and your company? (See Section A, below.)
- Identify the keys to success in your company, your department, and your team: What styles, attitudes, and accomplishments are typically rewarded in your company? Which work best with your management style? (See Section B, below.)
- Determine the essential functions of the position: What absolutely must get done in this job? (See Section C, below.)
- Consider which qualifications are necessary to do this job: Are certain skills, licenses, education, or experience required? (See Section D, below.)
- Decide whether any other information relevant to the job should be noted in the job description: If travel is required or the employee will have to be on call or work nights, for example, you will want to include that information. (See Section E, below.)

At the end of this chapter, you will find a Job Description Worksheet you can use to record this information as you prepare to write your job description. (The worksheet is also included in Appendix B and on the CD-ROM at the back of this book.) This will help you organize your thoughts and make sure that every important detail finds its way into the final document.

A. Consider the Big Picture

You may be wondering why you should start writing a job description for one position in one company by analyzing larger concerns, like the job market, the economy, and the competition. The answer is that those big-picture issues will aid you in determining what skills and abilities you'll need at your company, who may be available to fill the position, and who you will be competing with to hire them. In other words, taking a broad view will help you craft a job description that appeals to the people you really want to bring on board, and help ensure that you can land them.

As a line manager or HR professional, you may not get a lot of opportunities to step back and take a broader perspective—and chances to shape the future of your company probably seem few and far between. But even if you feel that you are not in a position to affect the big picture, your responsibility to write job descriptions gives you a lot more input than you might think. You are designing an organization, position by position, to accomplish specific things, both now and in the future. To do the job right, you need to know what your competition and the economy are doing.

This chart depicts the elements you should consider as you do this important design work. Everything outside the largest circle is part of the broader perspective that should inform your job descriptions.

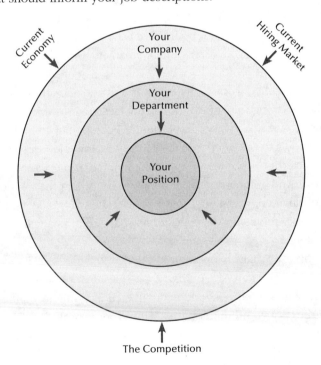

1. The Current Economy

The relationship between the job you are describing and the vagaries of the current economy is an important consideration as you go forward. While you don't have to dig deeply into Alan Greenspan's speeches on future interest rates, exuberance, and "bubbles," understanding how the economy affects the job market in your area will help you draft a job description that speaks to the applicants you're after.

> **EXAMPLE:** In the late 1990s and early 2000s, the Silicon Valley had a booming economy that was snapping up technology experts as soon as they had their degrees. Reports in major publications spoke of the urgent need for more and more computer science and information technology graduates. Some even made dire predictions that if this talent pool ran dry, American innovation would slow to a grinding halt.
>
> For the hiring manager, this environment posed extreme challenges. Because so many companies were fighting for the same applicants, managers had to make these kinds of jobs look more appealing than ever before. The compensation offered for these positions skyrocketed; companies offered new kinds of flexibility, benefits, and perks; and job descriptions were crafted to make these positions look like life-altering opportunities. The concept of a "work day" changed dramatically; it became a chunk of time that rarely took place during the daylight hours. Even the physical work environment at many companies changed to encourage creativity and allow workers to blow off steam.
>
> Managers also had to carefully consider the audience they were trying to attract when shaping the appearance of job descriptions and deciding where to post them. The scarce labor pool required companies to look outside the normal channels to find their talent. For the first time, job descriptions were routinely posted on websites—the perfect marketing mechanism for the wired world. And getting the target audience to look at the job descriptions required creative copy and bold graphics. Because of the economy of the times, job descriptions for these positions changed dramatically, both visibly and in content.

So how can you use what's happening in the economy as you put together your job descriptions? Here are some tips:

- Consider how the business and economic climate might require you to change the way you think about specific work getting done. Is the traditional nine-to-five workday the only way? Does it matter where the work is done? If the job is for a counterperson at a fast food restaurant, it does matter. If the job involves telemarketing, however, it could take place anywhere there is a telephone.

- Stay flexible in your thinking, so you can write a description that allows for creative and different ways to do things.
- Don't paint yourself into a corner by making the requirements of the job so specific that only a very small percent of the available applicant pool would be eligible.
- Factor in significant economic characteristics as you design the job. These might include things like:
  - a depleted or diminishing workforce—in this situation, you'll have to be very creative and flexible in creating a compelling position that stands out from the rest
  - a glut of available talent in your geographical area—this will allow you to be very specific in what you are seeking
  - lots of working parents—this might make it imperative to offer benefits like flexible work hours and telecommuting, and to highlight them in the job description.

2. The Current Hiring Market

Unlike the economy, which affects all positions and companies in some way, the current hiring market is typically specific to the kind of position for which you are hiring. Before you can write the description, you'll certainly want to know who is available to fill the job, where you're most likely to find them, and what you'll have to offer to land the right person. Here are some key issues to consider:

1. **How easy will it be to find the kind of people you are looking for to fill this job?** Ask others in your company, or your larger professional network, about their experiences in hiring for this type of job. Are candidates plentiful or scarce? Can you count on finding high-quality applicants, or will you need to set your sights a bit lower (or plan to take more time in filling the position)?

2. **Where are you going to find the best candidates—internal promotions, colleges, specific companies?** You'll want the look and content of your job description to fit the source from which you will most likely be filling the position.

3. **What are the current salary requirements for this type of position, considering the skills you need?** While few job descriptions actually lay out these numbers, you'll want to have them in your head as you "level" the position. In other words, if you will have to pay more than you can afford for a specific skill set, you may want to eliminate or change that requirement in your job description.

3. The Competition

No matter what type of business your company does, chances are good that you are in direct competition with someone else for the talent you need to fill your job. Sometimes that competition is obvious—say, between Microsoft and Sun, or Taco Bell and Kentucky Fried Chicken. But often, it is the less obvious competition that will keep you from landing the applicant you want. For example, you may have selected an ideal candidate after a long search, only to find that another company has offered that person more flexibility, better opportunities for growth, or a unique chance to learn something new.

Here are some of the different types of competition you will want to consider as you prepare to write your job description:

- **Industry-specific competition.** You probably know who your company competes with for revenue and customers. This competition often extends into the hiring realm as well. By pointing out what differentiates your company (and your position) from the competition in your job description, you can proactively address this issue.

  EXAMPLE: You own a car dealership, and often run into the dealer who sells the same make of cars in a neighboring town. You compete for customers on pricing and availability, you compete for radio airtime for your advertising, and you compete for the best-qualified job applicants, as well.

  You need a seasoned salesperson with experience in fleet sales to round out your sales team. You know (by poking around on its website) that the other dealer is hiring for the same kind of skill set. You have an opportunity, through your job description, to make your position more compelling to applicants. By adding a new responsibility (such as training for a management position), you can provide an opportunity that the other dealer has not.

- **Background-specific competition.** Many jobs require specific qualifications that apply across a number of industries. For example, a bookkeeper or certified public accountant can work for a number of different companies in most industries. If you are hiring for this type of position, you will encounter competition from many different industries, primarily from businesses that are nearby. So as you write your job description, consider whether neighboring companies are hiring for similar positions. (The best place to find this information is a company's website, if it has one.) Work to make your job sound more interesting than anything these other companies can provide. Be creative in what you can offer: Training opportunities, telecommuting, flexible hours, and so on can make a job much more interesting to a candidate.

• **Competing interests.** Competing interests are the specific factors that might play a role in a particular candidate's decision to apply for and accept a job. For example, a candidate might have family responsibilities that preclude travel or late hours, or have ambitions to move quickly up the company ladder. Often, the job itself is only one of your candidate's interests. These are much harder to ferret out ahead of time, as they are specific to each candidate. But you can prepare to deal with them by thinking about the requirements of the job. If you know which tasks are not negotiable (that is, you just can't change them, even for the right person) and which are open to discussion, you can figure out how to address competing interests appropriately as they come up.

At this point, you undoubtedly have some ideas about how the economic climate, the available pool of candidates for your position, and the competition might play into the way you craft your job description. Before continuing on to Section B, take a few minutes to write down your initial thoughts in the "Big Picture Considerations" section of the Job Description Worksheet.

B. Identify the Keys to Success in Your Company and Your Department

Most managers have had the unfortunate experience of hiring or promoting someone, only to later figure out that he or she just doesn't have what it takes. Besides eating up a lot of your time, these unsuccessful hiring moves can demoralize your team, set back your work, and reflect poorly on you as a manager.

Of course, the logical way to avoid this expensive and time-consuming problem is to hire or promote only people who do have what it takes! And the best way to do this is to spend some time thinking about which characteristics lead to success in your company and in your own department. By making this critical step a part of your preparation to write a job description, you are saving yourself tremendous time and effort down the road.

1. How Is Success Defined in Your Company?

As an employee of your company, you probably already have a good idea of what it takes to be successful there. To go beyond your own experience and perceptions, you can consider company statements and systems that reflect what the company is looking for in its employees, such as:

- the company's mission, vision, and values statements
- performance appraisal forms and procedures, and
- reward and recognition programs.

a. Mission, Vision, and Values Statements

To find out which accomplishments, skills, and attitudes your company holds in highest esteem, it's best to start by going straight to the horse's mouth: your company's own statements about its mission, vision, and values. Not every company has formal statements on these issues, but more and more see the advantages of spending some time and effort hammering out exactly what the company stands for.

If you're wondering about the purpose of these various statements or how they differ from each other, here's a quick primer.

- **A mission statement** is typically a very brief (often one sentence) description of the company's purpose. For example, the mission of Nolo, the publisher of this book, is to "provide do-it-yourself legal solutions for consumers and small businesses." If someone asked you to describe, in a sentence or phrase, why your company exists, your answer would most likely be your company's mission.

- **A vision statement** usually describes where the company is headed. Vision statements are often aspirational—that is, they describe the rosy future the company hopes to achieve, not its current state of affairs. For example, Toastmasters International, an association of clubs that help people improve their public speaking skills, seeks to empower people "to achieve their full potential and realize their dreams."

- **A values statement** typically describes the company's position on important issues, as well as the behaviors and character traits that the company would like its employees to aspire to. A values statement might be as simple as "customer service is our top priority," or it might take the form of a list of political and ethical beliefs. For example, the Body Shop, a company that sells lotions, soaps, and other beauty and health products, lists among its values "against animal testing," "defend human rights," and "protect our planet." Whether a statement or a list, the values statement is a great place to look for information on what the company wants from its employees.

Here are a few examples of how you can use your company's mission and vision statements to discern your company's criteria for success—and to draft a job description that will attract candidates who can meet those criteria.

- The mission of The Walt Disney Company is to be one of the world's leading producers and providers of entertainment and information. If you were writing a job description for a position within Disney, you might include a bullet point in the "Job Requirements" section that read something like, "A good sense of fun and the desire to entertain!"
- Google, the Silicon Valley internet search engine company, has a mission "to organize the world's information and make it universally accessible and useful." If you were writing a job description for a company with this type of mission, you should make clear that a grand sense of scale and a never-say-quit attitude is necessary for success.
- Newman's Own, Paul Newman's food conglomerate (from which Mr. Newman donates all of his profits to charity) describes its mission as "Shameless Exploitation in Pursuit of the Common Good!" Among the values you'd want to emphasize in a job description for this type of company are creativity, a sense of humor, and a desire to be socially responsible.

If your company has a values statement, that's an even more direct explanation of what the company is looking for. Corporate values statements are often very broad and pie-in-the-sky, so you may need to determine how the values are actually used (or not used) in your company. Are they a part of the performance review process? Do they factor into hiring, promotional, and disciplinary decisions? If your company's values look good on a website or coffee mug, but don't play a role in the day-to-day functions of the company, they won't give you much help in writing your job description.

If your company does not have a values statement. Many smaller and newer companies haven't taken the time to craft a values statement. But every company has values, whether or not they've been articulated in written form. Look at what types of behaviors and accomplishments bring rewards in your company, how the company treats its customers, and how the company wants to be known in the community. These are the values you should reflect in your job description.

Here are a couple of real-life examples of published values and some ideas about how you could incorporate those values into a job description:

- Charles Schwab, the investment brokerage, states on its website that it wants employees:
    - with the desire, drive and creativity to find solutions that help meet our clients' needs

- who want the chance to learn, grow with the company and explore their career opportunities
- who will strive for excellence in achieving our clients' and our company's goals
- with the highest ethical standards—individuals who take pride in making a difference in people's lives

Schwab is very explicit about the type of employees it wants—in fact, you could drop these values right into a job description with very little revision. (How to actually go about filling the job with a person who has these qualities is discussed in Chapter 5.)

- The DaimlerChrysler website lists five core values: innovation, sustainability, the environment, responsibility, and heritage. When you click on a value, you can see the specific company programs that support it. Because these terms are quite general, you can't simply copy them into your job description. Instead, you'll need to incorporate them into the job requirements section (and ask about them in the interview) by adding a bullet like "ability to work creatively to develop effective, innovative solutions" to show that innovation is important.

b. Performance Appraisal Documents

Nearly every company has some way of measuring how its employees are doing. This tool might be called a performance appraisal, a focal review, a performance evaluation, or something else (this book uses the term "performance appraisal").

A performance appraisal sets out the standards by which managers measure their employees. These standards may vary within work groups or job positions or may be the same across the whole company. Either way, they are a window into what the company values in its employees. By poking through your company's appraisal tool(s), you will have a pretty good blueprint for drafting your job description.

Performance appraisals typically list the employee's goals for the period under review, rate how well the employee did in reaching those goals, evaluate how the work was done (it's very helpful to see how this is measured), and set goals—or areas for improvement—for the next performance review period. Look closely at the goals for the position and how managers want those goals accomplished—for example, if a manager writes, "Jack consulted successfully with employees from outside of his department to develop marketing materials," you'll know not only that the job requires developing marketing materials, but that the ability to work collegially as part of a team is important as well.

Many companies use a performance appraisal document that outlines job competencies—skills that are necessary for a particular job. For example, a counter person at a fast food restaurant must have great customer service skills, be able to work quickly under pressure, and be able to use a cash register and make change. This translates neatly into job requirements for your job description. Analyzing how your company measures employee performance will give you valuable information about what it takes to be successful in a specific position.

c. Reward and Recognition Programs

Usually found in larger companies, reward and recognition programs provide great insight into what the company really values. These programs typically provide incentives and prizes to employees who reach certain milestones or meet specific goals. Familiarize yourself with what your company does in this area. Are there well-developed awards programs, or even informal kudos delivered for specific actions, accomplishments, or behaviors? If so, you can use this information in writing your job description.

> **EXAMPLE:** A large pharmaceutical company depends on receiving FDA approval at crucial stages in the development of its drugs. Because this approval is absolutely critical to the company's success, it has built specific rewards and recognition programs around these milestones.
>
> To use this information in your job description, you could include things like "must be able to meet deadlines consistently, and document findings thoroughly, in preparation for government review." This lets your job candidates know how important this is to the company—and how their performance will be measured if they accept the position.

Now it's time to turn to the Job Description Worksheet and fill out the section titled, "Success at Your Company."

2. How Is Success Defined in Your Department or Team?

As important as it is to know what your company values, it might be even more important to know exactly what you value in the people who work for you. After all, if you will manage the position for which you are writing a description, that employee's success will depend heavily on how well he or she works with you.

When delving into this area, you must remember to consider only work-related requirements, not personality traits. Through your experience as a manager, you may have found that certain things drive you crazy or hinder your working relationship with someone. Of course, you want to avoid hiring more people who are difficult for you to manage, but you must take care to avoid the legal pitfalls described in Chapter 2. As you read through this section, keep in mind that you must focus on work traits, not personality traits.

Here are a few examples of personality challenges, and how you can translate them into work-related requirements.

PERSONALITY CHALLENGES	DESIRED WORK TRAITS
Spends too much time asking questions.	Must be self-driven.
Focuses too much on how to do things rather than just getting them done.	Candidate should be strongly results oriented.
Unable to handle a variety of responsibilities at once.	Ability to multitask is crucial.
Tentative in meetings.	Strong ability to express views clearly and concisely.

Conversely, there may be a number of personality traits that you believe work very well with your management style. The rule remains the same: Keep the job description focused on the job itself. Flip the positive personality traits into work traits and list them in your job description.

PERSONALITY STRENGTHS	DESIRED WORK TRAITS
Great at speaking his/her mind.	Good communication skills, direct in dealings with others.
Energetic personality.	Ability to complete large amounts of work in short time frames.
Really good at figuring out next steps.	Must show initiative in accomplishing agreed-upon goals.
Dedicated, honest, high integrity.	Candidate should have proven, sustained record of high-quality work.

 EXERCISE 1:
BRAINSTORM WORK TRAITS

This exercise will help you figure out which work traits you want to attract—and which you want to avoid—through your job description. (You'll find a tear-out copy of this exercise in Appendix B.)

1. On the chart below, quickly write five positive traits—things that you like to see in your employees—on the plus side, and five negative traits on the minus side. It may help to think about the best person who has ever worked for you, and the worst—what made these employees good or bad?

+	−
1.	1.
2.	2.
3.	3.
4.	4.
5.	5.

2. Consider whether the characteristics you've listed are personality traits or work traits.
3. If they are work traits, write them down in the "Brainstorm Work Traits" section of the Job Description Worksheet.
4. If they are personality traits, write down three ways that each trait affects you or your team's work. Now you should be able to translate them into work traits and include them in your worksheet.

Personality Traits	How This Affects Our Work
1.	1. 2. 3.
2.	1. 2. 3.
3.	1. 2. 3.

This exercise will help you come up with a list of the key characteristics that work and don't work for you as a manager. By putting them into job-specific language, you can include them in your job description, and continue to use them throughout the life of the job. You have also identified keys to success in working for you directly, and you can use this over and over when you hire people, set their goals, and measure their performance.

C. Determine the Essential Functions of the Job

So far, you've been looking at factors that apply across positions—who's available in your area and industry, and what you and your company expect of employees, now and in the future. Now it's time to focus more narrowly on the position itself: What do you want the person in this position to do?

As a manager, you no doubt have a mental picture of what you would like the employee in this position to accomplish under your guidance. That image will be the basis for figuring out the essential functions of the job. This section explains how to turn your ideas into a list of essential job functions that will help you find the right employee—and keep your company out of legal trouble. Here are the steps you'll have to follow:

1. Brainstorm a comprehensive initial list of possible things that the person in this position could do.
2. Prioritize your list, determining which tasks are most important and why.
3. Eliminate the lower priority items.
4. Test your modified list to make sure your thinking is sound, legal, and fair.

(See Chapter 2, Section A, for more information on the importance of identifying essential job functions.)

1. Create an Initial List of Job Functions

There are a number of ways to come up with your initial list of job functions. It may already be so clear in your head that all you have to do is start writing. You may be a fan of the "mind mapping" method where you start with a central concept, and branch off different related ideas from there to create a pretty comprehensive list. Or you may be the master of the blank page, an inviting space to capture your entire creative process.

EXERCISE 2:
BRAINSTORM JOB FUNCTIONS

Use this exercise to come up with a list of job functions and begin to figure out which tasks are most important.

1. Give yourself exactly five minutes. In the space below, write down everything that you need the person in this job to do. When your five minutes are up, set aside the list.

   Things I NEED this person to do

   _____

   _____

   _____

   _____

   _____

   _____

   _____

   _____

2. Set your watch for five more minutes. The topic is, "What do I want the person in this job to do?" When your time is up, set aside the second list.

   Things I WANT this person to do

   _____

   _____

   _____

   _____

   _____

   _____

   _____

   _____

3. Take five more minutes to jot down ideas on this topic: "What are other people expecting from the person in this job?"

   Things OTHERS need this person to do

   _____

   _____

   _____

   _____

   _____

   _____

   _____

   _____

4. Now look at your three lists. In the "Job Functions" section of the Job Description Worksheet, write down any tasks that overlap and the number of times they overlap. List all of the remaining items at the end. You now have a fairly complete list of job functions, and the start of a prioritization process!

Save the editing for later. This chapter requires you to brainstorm and gather information—and the best way to do that is to write quickly and creatively, without worrying about spelling, grammar, or how your ideas will sound upon further reflection. Chapter 4 explains how to turn your creative language into a professional and polished job description.

2. Prioritize Your List

When you prioritize job functions, you'll need to figure out not only which tasks are most important, but also the reasons for your ranking—why these tasks are essential. Prioritization will require you to pare down your initial list—and if, like most managers, you have many things that need to get done, you'll have to be ruthless.

The next exercise will help you rank your priorities. You'll "grade" each item on your brainstorm list to designate its importance. To come up with the final list for your job description, you'll remove all but the top ten to 12 items. As you go through this exercise, make some notes about why you consider certain tasks more important than others. You'll use these notes later to make sure these functions are essential.

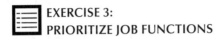

EXERCISE 3:
PRIORITIZE JOB FUNCTIONS

This exercise will help you pare down your list of job functions to the most important priorities.

1. On the Job Description Worksheet, write a letter grade next to each item on your complete list of job functions to indicate the item's relative importance. Items that are most important deserve an "A," while the least important should get a "C."

2. Consulting your graded list, jot a note next to each item about why you graded it as you did. Some of those reasons may include:

   a. Task is the reason the position exists.

   b. Task is best suited to being done by this position.

   c. Task would be nice to have but not critical.

   d. Task would be the _____ (second, third, fourth) thing I would need done right away.

   e. And so on.

3. Now, count your As (the most important rating). At this point, many managers will have either too many or too few "A" level tasks. As a rough guide, you should target ten to 12 tasks to list on your job description. In your mind, all ten or 12 should be absolutely crucial to the job.

4. If you have too many "A" items, repeat step 1 with only the items on your "A" list. Be ruthless, using absolute necessity as the litmus test. If the task is not absolutely necessary, it's a "B" or "C."

5. If you have too few "A" items, look at your "B" list. Which of those items are truly important to the job?

6. Once you've gotten your list down (or up) to ten or 12 items, list those on the Job Description Worksheet, under "Prioritized List of Job Functions."

Maybe you don't have a full-time position. If you can't come up with more than a few essential functions, you may need to reconsider whether this list comprises a full-time job. Can these functions be farmed out to your other employees? Or can you add new functions to create a full-time job? You might also consider creating a part-time position. Chapter 6 explains what to do if you're not sure whether you should create a full-time position.

Prioritization is a necessary evil that will make your job description much stronger. It could also lead to one of two outcomes:

1. **There may be too many functions that you want the person in this position to handle.** If that is the case, consider adding a "catch-all" bullet at the end of your list such as, "Additional responsibilities and tasks as necessary." This gives you the flexibility to add or subtract functions and tasks during the life of the job. Of course, if any of those additions become permanent, it's probably best to modify your job description to more accurately capture what is being done. And if you have such a long list that you don't think any one person can accomplish everything, you might also consider creating more than one position.

2. **You may feel like the job is too thin.** Were you too ruthless in paring down the tasks? Are you too close to the position to see something that you may have left out? Go back through your task list; ask someone else who knows something about the position to take a look as well. While you should not add fluff just to make the position sound meatier than it is, you should make certain that the important and critical functions are all there. And if you can't come up with enough work, you might be creating a part-time position.

3. Determine Which Remaining Tasks Are Essential

Now you have a prioritized list of tasks or functions, and a few notes about why each is important. But even though you know that these things are important to you, and you believe them to be critical to the job, that doesn't mean they qualify as "essential" for legal purposes.

As explained in Chapter 2, essential functions are the fundamental duties of the job: those things that the person holding the job absolutely must be able to do. The list of essential functions will determine your obligations towards applicants and employees with disabilities. If a function is truly essential, and the applicant or employee cannot do it with or without a reasonable accommodation, that person is not considered "qualified" for the job as a legal matter (and you don't have to worry about discrimination lawsuits based on your refusal to hire him or her). If, on the other hand, a function is not essential, an employee's or applicant's inability to do it because of a disability cannot legally play a role in your hiring decision.

💡 **You can include nonessential functions in the description, but you must designate them as such.** The purpose of listing essential functions, as noted above, is to make it easier for you and for applicants with disabilities to determine whether they are qualified for the position. Of course, this doesn't mean that you can't include less important functions in the descriptions, or tasks that you would like the person in the position to perform, even if they aren't absolutely necessary. Keep in mind, though, that you'll have to stand by your designations. If your job description says a task is not essential, you could be in legal trouble if you refuse to hire a disabled applicant because he or she cannot perform that task.

With these rules in mind, ask the following questions about each prioritized function:

1. Could this job be performed adequately without this function or task? (If the job exists precisely to perform that function, then the answer is "no.")
2. Could this task be performed easily by other employees or by someone in a different position?
3. Could this task be performed by someone without specialized skills, expertise, or other qualifications?

If your answer to all of these questions is a resounding "NO!" then your job task is essential and should stay in the job description. If you answered "yes" to any question, think harder about whether or not to designate it as an "essential function" in your description. It doesn't mean that the function absolutely can't be done by the person in this job; it just means that you should not list it as an essential function. Once you've finished this process, indicate which tasks are essential by marking an "E" next to each essential job function on the Job Description Worksheet.

D. Determine Qualifications

To complete this section of your job description, you'll need to know the qualifications necessary to do the job. Qualifications usually fall into one of these four categories:

- educational requirements (such as advanced degrees)
- training requirements (such as certificates or licenses)
- knowledge requirements (skills, abilities, familiarity with particular tools, languages, or software programs), and
- specific experience necessary to do the job.

1. Educational Requirements

Educational requirements may seem fairly straightforward, but you can get your company into trouble if you list requirements that aren't truly necessary. Of course, some positions absolutely require a particular degree. For example, a lawyer must have a Juris Doctor (JD) to do his or her job. Likewise, you would want your doctor to have an MD.

But other educational requirements (such as a college degree) may not be necessary if a person with equivalent experience could do the job just as well. This applies even to technical educational requirements, such as a degree in computer science. And because a degree requirement like this could screen out disproportionate numbers of applicants in certain protected classes, it might be discriminatory.

Unless the job really does require a higher degree, you should add the words, "or equivalent experience" to the requirement. The entire line would read either "College Degree preferred" or "College Degree or equivalent experience required." Of course, you can note a specific degree if that is necessary, such as "Bachelor of Science, Biology preferred."

2. Training Requirements

Many jobs require particular certifications, licenses, or training courses. Examples include certification for certified public accountants (CPAs), real estate licenses, pilots' licenses, Microsoft certifications, and any specific mechanical or tool-related training. Like educational requirements, you should make sure that any licensing or training you require is truly necessary to do the job.

3. Knowledge Requirements

Most positions require certain skills and abilities—for example, the ability to generate spreadsheets using a particular type of software, the ability to work quickly and with minimal supervision, leadership skills, the ability to type 50 words per minute, or fluency in French or COBOL. Some of these will fit within the essential functions of the job, and you can list them there (for example, "Must generate Excel spreadsheets weekly to track product sales"). Other requirements apply more broadly across a job's essential functions (for example, "Skill in resolving conflicts and gaining cooperation among competing interest groups"). These types of requirements can be listed in the "Knowledge Requirements" section of the job description. As always, you must be able to show that these skills are necessary to do the job.

⚠ **Don't make assumptions.** Managers get in trouble when they assume that applicants of a particular nationality, gender, or other protected group are more or less likely to have certain abilities. Your job description will help you avoid these problems by identifying the particular skills necessary to do the job, but you must do your part by setting aside any stereotypes you might hold. Do you believe that older people don't understand computers; that women can't use power tools; or that someone with a Latino surname speaks fluent Spanish? These are the types of beliefs that will prevent you from finding the most qualified candidate—and possibly land your company in court.

4. Experience

This is where you list job-related experience, such as "Five to seven years of managerial experience a plus," or "Proven results in outside sales." Be careful in listing a specific number of years, as everyone learns at different speeds and you might be eliminating potentially great candidates by being too specific.

List each required qualification in the appropriate category in the "Qualifications" section of the Job Description Worksheet.

E. Other Requirements

The last section in your job description is where you should list anything else that job applicants should know but that doesn't fit in other sections of the description. Examples include travel requirements, any physical requirements of the job (remember that these must be essential tasks to avoid disability discrimination), unusual business hours, on-call requirements, and so on. While you may be tempted to throw in the kitchen sink here, that's not a good idea. A good rule of thumb is to include anything you think an applicant needs to know in order to make an informed decision about taking the job—that is, anything that, if an applicant learned it later, might cause him or her to turn down your offer.

List any additional information applicants need to know in the "Other Requirements" section of the Job Description Worksheet.

Test Your Knowledge

Questions

1. In defining your job, which of the following do you not need to consider?
   - A. Current economy
   - B. Current hiring market
   - C. College graduation rates
   - D. The competition

2. In considering potential competitive influences on the position you are defining, you should:
   - A. Not worry about other companies
   - B. Consider personal interests
   - C. Draft a competitive analysis
   - D. Increase your salary offer

3. Company values rarely factor into hiring decisions.
   - A. True
   - B. False

4. Which of the following should not be considered in determining how your company defines success?
   - A. Company mission and values
   - B. Rewards programs
   - C. Termination reasons
   - D. Performance appraisal tools

5. Which of the following would be a personality strength rather than a desired work trait?
   - A. Motivated self starter
   - B. Results oriented
   - C. Honest and fair
   - D. Strong communicator

6. If you cannot easily translate a personality trait or challenge into a work trait, you should:
   - A. Include it in your description as is
   - B. Leave it out

7. When brainstorming a list of essential job functions, you should write down only the first ten to twelve things that come to mind.
   - A. True
   - B. False

8. In order to figure out which job functions are the most important, you should:
   - A. Consider what needs to get done
   - B. Add things you'd like to get done
   - C. See what makes others successful
   - D. Accommodate the disabled

9. If a function is not completely necessary to the business, you can include it in your job description as long as you note that it isn't essential.
   - A. True
   - B. False

10. You will always have to follow all of the steps outlined in this chapter to write a legally defensible job description.
    - A. True
    - B. False

Answers

1. **C. College graduation rates.** Considering the current economy, the current hiring market, and the competition is usually sufficient to write a good job description.

2. **B. Consider personal interests.** Often you will be competing with an individual's other interests or job offers in the job search process. Keep your job description flexible enough to allow for these considerations.

3. **False.** Company values are a great way to determine what skills and characteristics will make employees successful.

4. **D. Termination reasons.** The other choices are very useful tools to determine what a company values; termination reasons will be less useful, because they are often specific to the employee who has been terminated.

5. **C. Honest and fair.** While we would all like our employees to have this personality trait, it doesn't belong in a job description because it is not specifically related to the work.

6. **B.** Leave out anything that is not work-related.

7. **False.** Brainstorming is a time to go crazy with everything you can think of that you would like to include in the job. You'll have ample opportunity as you prioritize to cut your list down to ten or 12 items.

8. **A.** Consider what needs to get done. The operative word here is "needs." In order to be an essential function of a job, the function must be truly necessary.

9. **True.** As long as you indicate that the function isn't essential, you can include it in the description. But you can't refuse to hire a disabled applicant just because he or she can't perform one of these functions.

10. **False.** As you become more and more comfortable writing job descriptions, you can take shortcuts in this part of the process.

JOB DESCRIPTION WORKSHEET

Division/Department:	
Location:	
Job title:	
Reports to:	Title:

BIG PICTURE CONSIDERATIONS

1. State of the current economy:

2. Current hiring market:

3. Competition:

SUCCESS AT YOUR COMPANY

1. Mission, vision, and values:

2. Standards measured in performance appraisal tools:

3. Accomplishments noted in reward and recognition programs:

SUCCESS ON YOUR TEAM

Positive Work Traits

1.

2.

3.

4.

5.

Negative Work Traits

1.

2.

3.

4.

5.

JOB FUNCTIONS

•	•	•
•	•	•
•	•	•
•	•	•
•	•	•
•	•	•
•	•	•
•	•	•
•	•	•

Next to each function, write a letter grade indicating importance, "A" being most important and "C" being least important.

PRIORITIZED LIST OF JOB FUNCTIONS

•	•	•
•	•	•
•	•	•
•	•	•

List the ten to 12 most important functions, and designate essential functions with an "E."

QUALIFICATIONS

Education:

Training (licenses, programs, or certificates):

Knowledge Requirements:

Experience:

OTHER REQUIREMENTS

Chapter 4

Writing the Job Description

Grab your pen and paper, computer, or whiteboard, because it's time to sit down and write the job description. In this chapter, you'll learn the Golden Rules for writing job descriptions, strategies for coming up with precise and compelling language, and tips on reviewing your draft for legal pitfalls and other potential problems. This chapter also explains how to get and use relevant input from others, to make certain that your job description reflects the needs of everyone who will work with the person in that position.

In the last chapter, you learned how to gather the information necessary to create an effective description. You should now have a good sense of the job market and competition, what it takes to succeed in the job you are defining, and even a little bit about what it takes to be successful working with you. You should also have a brainstormed list of job functions, requirements, and other information. Now it's time to turn all of this information into a clear and compelling job description, using a few golden rules, some simple language skills, and a lot of examples.

Some say that a job description should fit onto a single page. As the media for posting job descriptions change, however, this can be a tough rule to apply—for example, what constitutes a "piece of paper" when you're writing for the Web? A better rule is simply to say exactly what you need to say, no more and no less. In other words, write a focused, spare description that sells the job to the kind of candidate you want to attract.

Armed with your completed Job Description Worksheet from Chapter 3, samples of job descriptions (see Appendix C), and your best writing skills, you shouldn't have much trouble pulling together a good description. After all, you've already done a lot of the work!

 Remember the basic components of the job description. As explained in the Introduction, there are four basic sections of a job description:
- A brief summary of the job—it's easiest to write this last, although it appears first.
- A list of job functions and responsibilities, with the essential functions clearly spelled out.
- A list of requirements necessary to do the job.
- Any other information necessary to describe the job.

A. Five Golden Rules for Writing Job Descriptions

As you start writing the language for your description, keep these five rules in mind. Following them will help you write a legal, compelling, and effective description.

1. Stick to the Job

Everything in the description must be directly relevant to the job. For many managers, the job description becomes a wish list of skills or personality traits—what they like in a person—rather than a description of essential functions—what they need from the employee who will fill the position. For example, if you are considering writing a bullet point like "Sunny personality a must," is that absolutely necessary to do the job? Could someone who occasionally exits the bed on the wrong side do equally well in this job? And how do you plan to measure luminosity when it's time to do a performance evaluation? In this case, it's better to describe exactly what you need the person to do: "Excellent customer service skills are a must" or "Must be able to work successfully with employees from other departments" might be better descriptions, for example. As soon as you add a line to the description that doesn't relate directly to the job, you may be exposing your company to legal trouble.

> **EXAMPLE:** Stan is hiring for a counter person at his fast food franchise. He carefully writes up the job description so he can post it at the local high school. The job description includes many requirements that are directly to the job, including:
> - Basic math skills a must.
> - Cheerful, customer-focused demeanor necessary.
> - Able to multitask and operate under stress.
> - Good problem-solving skills.
>
> But then Stan gets to the portion of his job description that details the physical requirements of the job. He writes:
> - Must be able to stand all day.
> - Must be able to lift at least 30 pounds.
>
> In his mind, he's just describing the average counter person, who will stand much of the time, and will lift and carry boxes that could weigh a lot. However, Stan's description eliminates a portion of the workforce that could be well qualified for—and very successful at—the job, but would not be able to meet the standing and lifting requirements. With simple seating accommodations and some lifting assistance, those who cannot physically

stand all day and lift heavy boxes might be just as qualified as any other candidate. And because Stan's description unnecessarily screens out these applicants, it might also give rise to a disability discrimination claim.

To make sure your description includes only relevant, necessary requirements, consider these questions for each bulleted item:

- Is this absolutely necessary to do the job?
  - If the answer is yes, leave it in.
  - If the answer is no, you may just want to take it out. If the function is desired but not necessary, you might want to include it as a nonessential function. (See Section B2, below, for more on this.)
- Have you considered alternative ways to accomplish the same tasks or duties?
  - If there are multiple ways to do a particular thing, make sure that your job description focuses on the desired results, not the method of achieving them. In the above example, Stan really just wants someone who can serve customers for the whole length of a shift. Those were the desired results. Standing up all day is just one way to accomplish that.
  - If there are no alternatives, then it should stay in the description as is.

2. Be Clear

Overwritten or vague job descriptions are not effective tools for hiring or managing. Some managers try to make a job seem more important by using words that sound bigger and better. Instead of bringing in the best and brightest candidates, these types of descriptions leave everyone uncertain as to what the job really requires—and who should be applying for it. For instance, if you are describing a position that is responsible for telling other employees about important company news and developments, you could write:

- "This position is responsible for communicating and announcing any internal issues of importance to any of the constituencies involved in the company's day to day happenstances, in formats including, but not limited to, daily updates, weekly publications, monthly newsletters, and annual reports."

Not only does this description fail to describe what the position really does, but it also uses terms that might confuse potential applicants. For example, the term "annual reports" is commonly used to describe the lengthy, technically detailed documents a company has to prepare each year for its shareholders. If the position requires only an annual email or brief letter to employees informing them of the company's accomplishments for the past year, your effort to make the job more important probably succeeded—in scaring away applicants who might have been really good at this job.

Alternatively, you could write:

- "Handles internal communications regarding company decisions and accomplishments, on an as-needed basis.

In contrast to the first example, this more concise version tells applicants what they'll have to do: occasionally relate important company news to others in the company.

3. Be Reasonable

Make sure that you are not asking a future employee to do the impossible. Hopefully, you already decided, after doing the exercises in Chapter 3, on a reasonable combination of tasks for the position. But just in case, now's the time to make sure that your list is manageable. Do the following examples—taken from real job descriptions— seem reasonable to you?

- Successful candidate must be available and on call 24/7.
- Position requires ability to drive trucks for a minimum of 36 hours straight.
- Candidate should have testable MBA (Master's of Business Administration) knowledge levels and be able to apply them in a BA (Bachelor of Arts) world.
- Consistent, constant good humor a must!

As these examples demonstrate, it is very easy to slip an unreasonable request into a job description. It seems like consistent, constant good humor would be nice to have in the workplace. But it's a rare person who never succumbs to a less-than-cheerful mood. And how would you measure the candidate's ability to meet this requirement? To make sure that you're being reasonable, ask yourself what the desired result of the requirement is, and whether there are other, equally acceptable ways to accomplish the same thing.

Let's apply these tests to the other bullets above.

Successful candidate must be available and on call 24/7.

24/7 implies that it would never be acceptable for the employee to be off call or unavailable—not on weekends, holidays, anniversaries, or snow days. Perhaps what you are trying to say is that at certain, agreed-upon times in the employee's schedule, he or she needs to be available all day and night. A better way to write this in your job description might be:

- "Position requires on-call availability for 24-hour periods according to a set schedule," or
- "Position will have to be on call and available for two 24-hour days every other week."

Position requires ability to drive trucks for a minimum of 36 hours straight.
A minimum of 36 hours of nonstop driving puts unnatural, unsafe, and possibly illegal requirements on this employee. And really, the desired result is that the truck driver can adhere to agreed-upon delivery times. A better way to communicate this might be:

- "Position requires drivers to keep delivery commitments."

Candidate should have testable MBA (Master's of Business Administration) knowledge levels and be able to apply them in a BA (Bachelor of Arts) world.
This quote is a little bit silly, but the author clearly wants to say something here, besides just being clever. Although the author's intent is a bit difficult to discern, it seems that he or she is looking for creative, new, and sophisticated approaches to common business problems. A better way of putting that might be:

- "Candidate must be able to provide strategic solutions to standard business challenges."

Of course, this could be even further refined to explain what types of problems the company needs to solve—human resources issues, marketing dilemmas, or profitability concerns, for example.

4. Look to the Future

As explained in Chapter 3, the process of defining the position and writing your job description provides an ideal opportunity to look at your current team, look at your company's changing needs, and make certain that you are preparing your team to meet those needs. You can find information about upcoming changes from the following sources, among others:

- **Discussions with your boss.** Stay up to date on what he or she is trying to accomplish with the larger team.
- **Company meetings.** Typically, some time is spent on company goals or upcoming challenges that may have a direct impact on your team.
- **Cross-functional meetings.** Listen to your peers in other departments. How can you and your team work more effectively to meet their needs as well?
- **Changes in policies or laws.** Stay relevant in your field by keeping up to date on external forces that may require you to change how you do your work.

- **Memberships in organizations, networking groups, or professional societies.** Keeping your own skills and abilities updated by interacting with other
professionals in your field will keep you in touch with new methodologies,
tools, and trends.

5. Tell the Truth

Many managers are tempted to puff up a job description in order to make it sound
more attractive to candidates. The problem is, once you hire someone based on
that description, he or she will be quite disappointed to learn that the position
is not as advertised—and if that employee left a good job to come work for your
company on the basis of a less-that-honest job description, your company might
be facing a legal claim.

Applying the old fashioned value of honesty will help you avoid this problem—and ensure that you are creating a document that will accomplish your goals
with that position. The honesty test will differ depending on the type of job you're
describing. Some questions to ask yourself include:

- Does the candidate absolutely need that [skill, certification, availability,
educational background, and so on] to do the job well?
- Is the candidate really going to be spending a measurable amount of time
on each of the essential functions listed in the description?
- Is each of the essential functions true to the nature of the position—that
is, do they fit together logically, or are you just trying to make up for some
other deficiency on your team by asking this position to handle this task?
- Have you described the position's responsibilities truthfully, without exag-
gerating their importance or minimizing how much time will have to be
spent on paperwork, menial tasks, or other thankless labor?

Your questions to test for honesty will vary, but your commitment to being
truthful in the process is critical.

B. Write the Job Functions, Responsibilities, and Requirements

The first section of the job description is the job summary, but it's best to save that
for last, after you have something to summarize. Instead, it's easier to start by writing functions, responsibilities, and requirements—the basic nuts and bolts of the
description. To get these sections down in writing, you'll need to follow these four
basic steps:

1. Consult and update your worksheet of brainstormed and prioritized job functions.
2. Capture each concept in bullet form, with strong, compelling language.
3. Test your draft for potential legal and practical problems.
4. Finalize and review your bullets for tone, theme, and impact.

At the end of this chapter, you'll find a template you can use to create your job description. (The template is also included in Appendix B and on the CD-ROM at the back of this book.)

1. Step One: Use Your List of Job Functions

In the last chapter, you spent some time coming up with a list of job functions. Take another look at your Job Description Worksheet. Do these still feel like the right tasks for the position? Has anything else come up that should be added? Does anything seem like it doesn't really fit with this position? Review your list carefully to make sure that the functions still seem essential and complete.

> **EXAMPLE:** Tom manages the men's department in a large retail store. He needs to hire a sales associate who has experience selling certain designer lines. His starting list of job functions and responsibilities includes:
>
> - Customer service abilities required.
> - Must have working knowledge of specific designer lines, including Haggar, Dockers, and Sansabelt.
> - Must have eye for color and design, and ability to assemble outfits for customers, up-selling accessories along the way.
> - Inventory management knowledge required.
> - Must have direct marketing skills.
> - Knowledge of cash register and inventory systems required.
>
> It certainly looks like Tom has a good starting list, but as he reviews it in preparation to begin writing his job description, he realizes that Sansabelt has terminated its relationship with his store recently. The store has replaced that line with Palm Beach's brand of polyester pants, so Tom corrects that reference on his list.

2. Step Two: Create Bullets

Up to this point, we've been talking about concepts and ideas. Now, we're going to focus on the actual words you use to describe those concepts.

Finding the right words can be a delicate balancing act. You must write clearly and honestly, so applicants and employees will know exactly what the job entails. At the same time, however, you also want to market the job—to sell it to the applicants you want to attract. So while "strong people skills" may be exactly what you need, "measurable customer service experience resulting in increased sales" may be your final bullet.

Your ultimate goal is to describe what you need, in a way that is compelling to whoever may be reading your job description. This does not mean that you should "enhance" your job functions to the point where they no longer accurately reflect the actual work, but you should at least make them sound interesting.

Try your hand at turning the following sentence fragments into bullets that would be compelling in a job description. Once you're finished, continue reading to see some examples that we found compelling—and some tips on coming up with concise and accurate functions.

BASIC JOB FUNCTION	JOB FUNCTION AS IT WILL APPEAR IN JOB DESCRIPTION
Customer service abilities required.	
Must have working knowledge of specific designer lines including Haggar, Dockers, and Palm Beach.	
Must have eye for color and design, and ability to put together entire outfits, up-selling accessories along the way.	
Inventory management knowledge required.	
Must have direct marketing skills.	
Knowledge of cash register and inventory systems required.	

How does your first pass look? Would you be interested in the position you described? Here are some questions to consider as you review each function:

1. What are the desired results of the function?
2. How would you measure success in this particular function?
3. Are you using the strongest and best language you can in to describe this function?

With these questions in mind, consider one of the examples above, "Inventory management knowledge required." Is Tom just looking for someone who has this knowledge? Even those of us who don't have a retail background can discern that what Tom really wants is someone with the ability to manage inventory, keeping the right items in stock at the right times while taking steps to prevent loss. A more accurate statement of what he wants might be "Inventory control, market timing, and loss prevention experience."

Next, consider how you would measure success in this function. Is it enough for Tom to find someone with experience in managing inventory, or would he prefer someone who not only has experience, but has proven success in inventory management? What are the measures of that success? Typically, there are targets set in these areas on which sales people can be measured. You can use this information to further qualify this factor as follows: "Proven success in inventory control, market timing, and loss prevention, as demonstrated by the ability to meet set targets while maintaining sales goals." This opens the door during the interview process for Tom to ask about hard numbers and past performance, which should tell him whether the person has been good at inventory management. Adding the "while maintaining sales goals" reminds Tom's candidate that both functions of the job are important.

Now, consider whether you have chosen the best way to describe what you want. Tom chose this as one of the highest priorities of the position, so succeeding at this function is really important. To let candidates know this, Tom could change:

- "Proven success in inventory control, market timing, and loss prevention, as demonstrated by the ability to meet set targets while maintaining sales goals."
  to this:
  - "Unparalleled success in inventory control, market timing, and loss prevention, as demonstrated by the ability to exceed set targets while outperforming sales goals."

Now, as Tom tries to fill his position, applicants will know exactly what is expected of them and how their performance will be measured.

Including Nonessential Functions in Your Job Description

If you peruse enough sample job descriptions, you will often see a section called "Nonessential Functions or Responsibilities." While the language is unwieldy, it is clearly a nod to the Americans with Disabilities Act (ADA). The purpose of including this section is usually to cover other job duties that the hiring manager would like the position to handle, without unfairly screening out applicants who can't perform them because of a disability. (For more on nonessential functions and the ADA, see Chapter 2, Section A.)

If you include nonessential functions in a job description, you must be prepared to give them up. If you don't hire someone because he or she is unable to do these tasks because of a disability, you could be inviting a discrimination claim.

For this reason, some companies avoid using this category, and instead include catchall bullets to add functions to the job. By adding a bullet such as "other projects and responsibilities may be added at the manager's discretion," or "special projects as required," you leave yourself the flexibility to deal with changing work environments. Some companies opt for a very broad catchall statement, such as "the above description is intended to describe the general nature and level of work being performed by employees in this position. They are not intended to be an exhaustive list of all duties, responsibilities, and qualifications of employees assigned to this job."

Go back to the original example and give it another try with these questions in mind. Are your bullets becoming more accurate and more compelling?

It takes practice and creativity to change your simple brainstormed functions into a compelling and complete description of what you really want and need. And you need to balance strong, interesting language with accuracy, honesty, and common sense. Here's another example of how one of Tom's basic functions can be turned into a more accurate and interesting bullet point:

BRAINSTORMED FUNCTION:	DIRECT MARKETING SKILLS REQUIRED.
First Pass at bullet form:	*Candidate must posses direct marketing skills.*
What are the desired results?	That the candidate can use direct marketing to build a sustainable client base of repeat customers.
2nd Pass at bullet form:	*Candidate can show that he or she has built a sustainable client base through the use of direct marketing.*
How would you measure success?	By measuring repeat customers and the percentage of sales they represent.
3rd pass at bullet form:	*Candidate can show that he or she has built a sustainable client base, and increased sales to that base, through the use of direct marketing.*
Are you using the strongest and best language to describe this requirement?	Through the use of direct marketing, candidate must be able to build and measurably grow sales to a sustainable client base.

The final changes in the above example are mostly a matter of personal style, not content. By moving the phrase "direct marketing" to the beginning of the bullet, it becomes the focus of the function. It's also easier to understand.

Use your final draft to emphasize what makes employees successful at your company. As you tweak your language to make it stronger, you can use the work you did in Chapter 3 to identify qualities of successful candidates. By simply adding some qualifiers to different job functions, you can let applicants know what your company values. For instance, if strong relationships with existing customers is a company value, you could write something like: "Applicant will build and nurture strong customer relationships to achieve sales goals and inventory numbers."

EXERCISE 4:
CREATE COMPELLING BULLET POINTS

Now it's time to use what you learned in this section to turn some of your job functions into bullets that would be compelling in a job description. Write down one of the functions from your description in the first space on the chart. Use the remaining spaces to consider the results you want from the position, how you would measure success in that function, and how you can make your language more descriptive. Use the answers to each of these questions to make your job function more compelling. Your last pass should result in a strong, interesting bullet point that you can drop right into your job description!

BASIC JOB FUNCTION:	
What are the desired results of this function?	
Revised function that includes these results:	
How would you measure success at this function?	
Revised function that adds measures of success:	
Are you using the strongest, most descriptive language?	
Revised function that uses most descriptive language:	

Although you'll always want to use compelling language, you don't have to actively sell the job in every part of the description. Typically, the list of job functions is where you'll need to use your best persuasive writing. When you're describing job requirements, on the other hand, you don't have to consider exactly why you're looking for particular licenses or other qualifications. For example, you don't have to describe what someone should have learned from becoming a certified public accountant—simply stating that your future CFO must be a CPA is enough. The same is true of other basic requirements, such as travel or on-call obligations. You can just say "10% travel time required"; you don't have to explain all of the reasons why an employee might have to travel.

3. Step Three: Review Your Draft for Legal and Practical Problems

Once you have a concise list of job functions and requirements, written in a way that is compelling and interesting, it's time to make sure that you've anticipated potential legal and practical pitfalls.

a. Legal Considerations

As explained in Chapter 2, there are some basic legal rules every job description must follow:

- Don't discriminate.
- Don't undermine at-will employment.
- Don't make promises you can't keep.
- Don't violate applicants' privacy.
- Don't create overtime classification problems.

Hopefully, after reading Chapter 2, you've managed to avoid most of these problems. But just in case, let's go over a list of questions to consider after you have written the body of your job description.

ISSUE: DISCRIMINATION

Questions to Ask	Saying It Wrong	Saying It right
Are each of these bullets focused solely on the job?	• Must have cheerful, friendly demeanor.	• Demonstrably strong customer service skills.
Does your language refer to race, religion, or other protected characteristics?	• Required to work on Rosh Hosanna and Yom Kippur. • Travel schedule requires unmarried person.	• Schedule may require holiday work. • 60%–75% travel.
Is your language gender specific?	• Prior experience as Waitress required.	• Prior experience as Waitperson required.
Does your language imply any preference for age?	• Boundless energy and stamina necessary.	• Ability to achieve set goals in timely fashion.
Are each of your bullets absolutely essential to the functions of the job?	• May be asked to help with inventory, requiring heavy lifting.	Delete bullet altogether – don't try to anticipate job functions that may not be necessary (essential).
Do your bullets describe the results you desire (good), or do they describe how to achieve the results (bad)?	• Must be able to stand at deli counter for duration of shift.	• Provide excellent service to customers at the deli counter.

ISSUE: AT-WILL EMPLOYMENT

Questions To Ask	Saying It Wrong	Saying It right
Is there anything in your job description that might lead job applicants to believe they will have job security?	• This is a permanent position.	• Leave it out. Don't say anything about duration, unless the position is temporary.
Is there anything that would lead applicants to believe that they would be fired only for specific reasons?	• Our company prides itself on our employee retention.	Nothing. Don't say anything that implies ongoing employment.
Have you promised raises or promotions?	• Demonstrated performance will be rewarded.	Again, nothing. Don't say anything about pay increases or other ways to reward performance in the job description.

ISSUE: IMPLIED CONTRACTS (Making Promises You Can't Keep)

Questions To Ask	Saying It Wrong	Saying It right
Did you put anything in the job description that may not actually happen (for any possible reason)?	• Success in first six months will lead to new training opportunities.	You could either omit this entirely, or say: • Training opportunities may be available.
In your zeal to make the job look attractive, have you crossed the line between truth and false statements?	• Position supervises a staff of trained professionals.	• Position is responsible for managing our intern program.

ISSUE: PRIVACY

Questions To Ask	Saying It Wrong	Saying It right
Does your job description include any references to candidates' private lives?	• Ability to function without sleep a must!	• Work schedule may require nighttime hours
Do you mention marital status?	• Looking for single, young achievers, ready to devote all of their energy to the job.	Nothing. Focus on the results you want applicants to achieve.
Do you refer to the applicant's political opinions?	• Candidate must have a "red state" sensibility.	• Candidate must be able to write political commentary for a primarily liberal audience.
Do you make any reference to off-duty conduct?	• Candidate must not have other work commitments.	• This is a full-time position.

ISSUE: OVERTIME CLASSIFICATION PROBLEMS

Questions To Ask	Saying It Wrong	Saying It right
Does the description lock the company into paying (or not paying) overtime?	• Required to supervise two employees, with authority to hire and fire.	• Will supervise Accounts Payable department.
Have you included any references to exempt/non-exempt status without running it by an expert?	• Eligible for overtime pay. • This is an exempt position. • Salaried position of $42,000 annually.	Don't discuss overtime: use words like hourly or salaried, or put salary information in the job description without an expert opinion.

b. Practical Considerations

To make sure you haven't inadvertently created any practical problems, test your description against the five golden rules explained in Section A. These rules will help you make sure that your description is effective, easy to understand, and easy to use in the future.

The legal review in Subsection a, above, already covered some practical concerns. For example, testing your description to make sure it doesn't discriminate against disabled applicants will require you to make sure that every function in the description is essential and relevant to the job. Here are a couple of additional things you'll want to look for:

- **Clarity.** Now that you've spent some time building up your bullets to attract the perfect candidate to your job, it's time to make sure you haven't gone overboard. Does your writing appear flowery? Do you have excessive words where one will do? Does the tone of your draft seem more like advertising than description? These are just a few clues that you might have gone a bit too far in your efforts to build up the job. You may need to go back and make sure that your description is clear and concise.

- **Future needs.** Has your job description captured not only the current functions of the job, but also those that will be necessary for success in the future? This is your chance to fill the job with someone who can take your team to the next level. Go back to the work you did in the last chapter. Does the description line up fairly well with the company vision? Are there any technological or other changes in the works that may impact how the job gets done? How about changes to accepted standards or laws? Keeping up with what is going on in your company and in your profession is critical to defining jobs, and ensuring success in your team.

4. Step Four: Finalize and Review for Tone, Theme, and Impact

In the haste of checking things off of your to-do list, it's easy to forget this final review. But it's important to take a step back and review the overall tone, theme, and impact of your description.

a. Tone

Tone refers to the general quality or effect of a document. When you are reviewing for tone, put yourself in the shoes of the reader. Does the description sound abrupt? Exaggerated? Matter-of-fact? Boring? Too good to be true? Or have you succeeded in making the position sound interesting, dynamic, and realistic? You can change the tone of a document by playing with some of the adjectives, the length of each bullet, or the order of importance. The important thing is to decide how you want your job description to be received, and to enforce that perception through your language.

b. Theme

A theme is an implicit or recurrent idea. Although an interesting theme can really spice up creative writing, you must make sure that you haven't allowed any negative themes to slip in accidentally. Does your document display emotions such as frustration or anger? Are you using the same words or phrases over and over? If so, what do these words convey? The universal theme for job descriptions should be an honest, accurate portrayal of the job—one that doesn't inadvertently hint that your company is understaffed, that your budget is insufficient to meet your team's needs, or that you don't feel supported by senior management, to name just a few things you'll want to keep out of the description.

c. Impact

Impact, like tone and theme, is usually in the eye of the beholder. After you've spent some time writing the job description, it can be tough to get the distance you need to figure out what kind of impact it will have on a reader. It's a great idea to have others review your work, especially someone in the same field as the position you're describing. Ask your readers questions like: "Does this description make you more or less interested?" "Do you want to find out more about the position?" "Do you question anything in the job description?" Pay attention to their answers. It is important that your job description have the proper and appropriate impact: compelling enough to attract the right person, but not so compelling that it sounds too good to be true.

C. Write the Job Summary

The very first thing anyone will read in your job description is the opening statement or job summary: a few short sentences explaining what the job is. Much like the first paragraph of a newspaper or magazine article, this paragraph will either leave your readers wanting more or leave them cold.

A less ominous way to think about the opening statement is as an "elevator pitch." The idea is to create a short description of the job that you could relate during a one-floor elevator ride. You want it to be informative and interesting, as well as short and punchy.

As you will see in the samples below, people call this opening statement all sorts of different things: a job summary, primary functions, job purpose, or general purpose.

No matter what you call it, the opening statement serves the same purpose: to provide a brief, compelling description of the most important aspects of the job. In writing your job summary, you want to:

- briefly describe the most important functions of the job
- explain how the job fits into the overall organization, and
- compel the reader to move on to the body of the job description.

By now, you are so familiar with the job that this step should come fairly easily. You can review the samples below to get you started. Here are some tips to keep in mind as you work on a draft:

1. Keep it brief—no more than about 75 words, or the length of a short elevator ride.

2. Use sentences, not bullet points. The style here differs from the body of your job description, as you want it to draw the reader in. The best way to do that is by using a conversational style, not sentence fragments. You'll see that some of the samples below do not use full sentences—and you'll probably also notice that those examples are not quite as compelling as the others.

3. Write two or three quick drafts. Are you using the same points in each? Or have you written three different things? If your drafts differ substantially, it's time to review how you've prioritized the job's functions. The most important functions should be reflected in the opening.

SAMPLE OPENING STATEMENTS

CORRECTIONS OFFICER

Primary Function: Perform duties assigned in the areas of legal process, including general custodial and detention functions essential to the operation of the detention center. Responsible for performance of dispatching functions as required and assigned. Ensure that the detention center is operating in a peaceful manner.

WATERSHED MANAGER

Summary: This position is responsible for monitoring, managing, and maintaining the Association's lakes, ponds, streams, and watershed including water quality and erosion control and related issues.

WEB DESIGNER

Summary: The Web Designer will have overall responsibility for working on a variety of projects primarily involved in website design and development, including creation of custom graphics. Responsible for designing the user interface and overall customer experience for our websites and applications. This includes overall navigation flow, layout of specific pages, and creation of individual graphic elements.

WELDER

Job Summary: Responsible for various types of weld preparation, welding, and weld finishing operations to manufacture product to customer drawings, specifications, or other forms of instruction.

ACCOUNTANT I

General Purpose of the Position: Process payroll. Help with filing taxes. Process purchase orders and other miscellaneous tasks related to accounting.

HOST/HOSTESS

Position Summary: Warm, friendly, immediate greeting to guests at the door. Seats and presents clean menus to guests in a friendly, professional, and quick manner.

MANAGER OF INFORMATION SYSTEMS

Purpose of Position: To perform in a pleasant, professional, and efficient manner a combination of duties mainly related, but not limited to, the creation and maintenance of the AS/400, PC, and phone systems.

MUSIC THERAPIST

Position Summary: The Music Therapist reports to the Director of Activities and is responsible for assisting in the planning and implementation of an ongoing program of musical activities designed to meet the interest and the physical, mental, psychological, and spiritual needs of each resident.

PRESIDENT/CEO

Job Purpose: The President is responsible for providing strategic leadership for the company by working with the Board and other management to establish long-range goals, strategies, plans, and policies.

Although each of these samples represents a very different job, they have a few things in common:
1. Each statement is short and to the point.
2. Each statement gives a basic overview of the job.
3. Each statement uses simple, clear language.
4. Each statement says a lot in very little space.

Using these examples as guidelines, go ahead and craft a short statement describing the essence of your job. When you've finished, you'll want to make sure it meets the legal and practical tests described in Section B3, above. But most of all, you'll want to put it to the test of common sense: does this statement reflect what you want the position to do?

D. Gather Input on Your Job Description

Chapter 1 discussed the importance of gathering input from others who will interact with the position you are describing. Now that you have a near-final job description, it's a great idea to ask for more feedback from the people who will deal with this employee. The most effective way to get useful feedback (as opposed to the time-honored metric of "thumbs up!") is to attach a brief list of questions to help respondents formulate their thinking.

Remember this graphic?

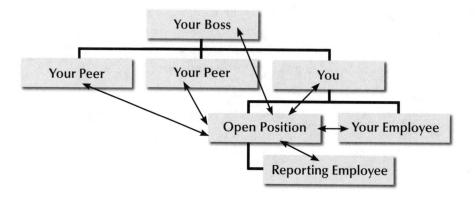

It's a simple way of demonstrating that many other positions will interact with the one you are describing. Ideally, you would get input from all of these people, but that is not always practical. Pick a few that will have the most interaction with this position. Give them a copy of the job description and attach a list of questions, such as:

1. Does the summary capture the essence of the job?

2. Are there any significant functions or responsibilities that I've left out?

3. Do these responsibilities and requirements seem reasonable for this position?

4. Would you respond positively to this job description?

By focusing the feedback and keeping the question list short, you will make it quick and easy for others to participate. You'll also help ensure that the feedback you get is useful and relevant. Once you've gathered this information, incorporate any comments that will make your job description stronger.

Don't forget your legal or HR department. This book is written to give you the information you need to vet your job description for potential legal and other problems. In many companies, however, the legal department or human resources is responsible for reviewing job descriptions and other personnel documents. If this is true in your company, you'll certainly want to run your final draft by the right people, to make sure that you haven't missed anything. And even if this type of review isn't required, it makes sense to take advantage of your in-house legal expertise (if your company has a legal staff) as you finalize your description.

Test Your Knowledge

Questions

1. Which of the following is not one of the basic sections of a job description?

    A. Job requirements   B. Salary ranges

    C. A job summary   D. Job responsibilities

2. When writing a job description, you should:

    A. Tie everything to the job

    B. Add jazzy words to market your position

    C. Be reasonable in what you are requiring

    D. Pay attention to future considerations

3. When beginning to write your job description, you should consult the Job Description Worksheet.

    A. True   B. False

4. Your job description should clearly spell out how you would like the work accomplished.

    A. True   B. False

5. In writing a compelling bullet for your job description, what do you *not* need to think about?

    A. The desired results   B. Whether the job will require overtime pay

    d. How you measure success   d. The language you use

6. In the "Other Information" section of your job description, it is important to use language that accurately markets the job and makes it attractive.

    A. True   B. False

7. Which of the following is not a basic rule when considering the legal aspects of your job description?

    A. Don't discriminate

    B. Don't undermine at-will employment

    C. Don't require previous experience.

    D. Don't violate applicants' privacy

8. It is okay to describe your position with gender-specific titles.

    A. True   B. False

9. If your company typically provides annual increases, you should mention that in your job description.

    A. True   B. False

10. You should run your final job description by others who will work with the position, to make sure you haven't left anything out or asked for too much.

    A. True   B. False

Answers

1. **B. Salary ranges.** There will be plenty of time throughout the hiring process to discuss salary, and doing so in a job description may be considered an implied contract.

2. **A, C, and D.** Although it's always a good idea to make your position sound compelling, don't go overboard with the sales pitch. If your "jazzy" language is inaccurate or misleading, you could get into trouble.

3. **True.** The worksheet you completed in the last chapter is designed to be great preparation for sitting down and writing your job description.

4. **False.** The job description is not about how the work is accomplished, but what needs to be accomplished. Focus on the results, and you won't inadvertently discriminate against any protected classes.

5. **B.** Will the job require overtime pay? There is no need for you to consider this as you write your job description. In fact, if you do, you may shade your description one way or the other, rather than keeping it objectively focused on the job at hand. Let the legal or HR experts classify your job for you.

6. **False.** The other information section is just a list of things that are pertinent to the job, such as travel requirements or on-call duties. The language here can be spare and informative.

7. **C.** You certainly should ask about a candidate's prior experience.

8. **False.** Waitresses become waitpersons, and stewardesses are flight attendants.

9. **False.** Mentioning an annual increase in a job description may lead to an implied contract, and jeopardize at-will employment.

10. **True.** Your colleagues can give you great feedback on your job description—it never hurts to have a second set of eyes.

YOUR COMPANY
JOB DESCRIPTION

| Job title: |
| Location: |
| Division/Department: |
| Reports to: Title: |

JOB SUMMARY

ESSENTIAL FUNCTIONS

-
-
-
-
-
-
-
-
-
-
- Other projects and responsibilities may be added at the company's discretion.

JOB REQUIREMENTS AND QUALIFICATIONS

Education:

Training Requirements (licenses, programs, or certificates):

Knowledge Requirements:

Experience:

OTHER INFORMATION

Special Information (Travel required, physical requirements, on-call schedules, and so on):

-
-
-
-
-

Chapter 5

Using Job Descriptions

Now that you have written a superb job description, it's time to put it to use! Chapter 1 explained how a job description comes into play throughout the "life cycle" of a job. It's a great hiring tool to advertise the opening, and it sets up baseline expectations for your new hire. You can use it measure and manage performance, set pay levels, determine whether discipline is needed, and document accomplishments. And the job description can limit your company's legal exposure by stating, clearly and legally, exactly what the candidate will be required to do.

This chapter explains how to use the job description for a number of practical purposes, including:

- job postings
- setting pay scales
- interviewing
- new employee orientation, and
- performance management.

You'll soon see that the time and energy you spent writing the description will be repaid in more efficient hiring and management.

A. Job Postings

When you use your description to post the job, you are actively selling the position in order to fill it with the best candidate. With this goal in mind, you will need to focus on those elements of the job that are the most important to you—in other words, which will be the real "deal-makers" or "deal-breakers." With your job description in hand, you have all the material you need to post the job or write an ad. In fact, your biggest problem will probably be to cut down your document to fit the available space. In the world of job postings, especially on the Internet, you won't be nearly as constrained as you would be in writing a more traditional help wanted ad for the newspaper, but the writing process for either of these types of postings are the same:

- **Prioritize the job functions.** Put the most important aspects of your job first.
- **Streamline your prose.** Make your writing simple and clear, using action verbs and punchy language to sell the position.
- **Remove inside information and company lingo.** Strip out any jargon or other "company-speak" information (such as obscure acronyms or product references). Also, make sure you take out any confidential information that you may have included for another use of the job description.

- **Describe your company.** Add a small paragraph on the company you work for, outlining the advantages of working there and a brief description of what the company does.
- **Close by explaining how to apply.** Leave room at the end to let candidates know what to do if they are interested in the position.

Job postings typically appear on job websites, bulletin boards (electronic and the old fashioned kind that require actual pins), and internal job opening lists. The posting rules vary depending on where you choose to post, so your first step is to familiarize yourself with those rules.

Check out the competition. Spend some time on Monster (www.monster .com) and Hot Jobs (www.hotjobs.com) to get a sense of what some actual postings look like, particularly in the field for which you're hiring. Have they sold the job well? Would you be interested in applying? Is there anything in the language of the job posting that you really like or dislike?

Of course, you can also list a job opening in traditional help-wanted advertisements, which typically appear in newspapers. However, as more and more of us move to the Internet as our primary source of current news and information, newspaper ads are starting to lose their popularity. And there are a number of advantages to using a job posting rather than a help-wanted ad, including:

- **The ability to target your audience better.** By choosing a posting site that is directly related to the nature of the job you are posting, you will know that qualified candidates are viewing your position. For example, by posting a job on www.nbmbaa.org (the National Black MBA Association), you are directly targeting African-Americans with MBAs. Likewise, many professions have umbrella organizations, such as the American Accounting Association (www.aaahq.org), a great place to recruit for accountants.
- **More space for selling your job.** Because space on the Web is unlimited, you can post much more information about your position on the Web or on an electronic bulletin board than you could in a newspaper ad. But this doesn't mean you should throw in as much information as possible. As we all know from our own reading habits, if you haven't hooked the reader in the first paragraph, they are never going to get to the information you've included on the third or fourth page, no matter how interesting you might find it to be.

- **The capacity to reach a much broader audience.** Help-wanted ads typically run in newspapers with specific and limited geographical reach. Web postings, in contrast, are accessible to anyone with a computer.

Help-wanted ads work for some jobs. When you're deciding how and where to post your job, consider the type of people whom you want to attract. If you're recruiting for a position that doesn't use or require computer skills, for example, you might have trouble reaching your target audience on the Web. And if you're looking for particular types of local talent—craftspeople, artists, or contractors, for example—you might get a lot of responses by posting your job on a bulletin board at a local lumberyard or arts supply store. If there's a local college or university that offers a degree program in the field you want, posting with the school's career office might yield great results.

1. Determine Your Priorities

To start turning your job description into a document that will attract the right people to apply, you need to prioritize the job functions. This will tell potential applicants what your company really needs out of this position.

To show you how to begin, we'll use the rather plain job description below as an example.

JOB DESCRIPTION

POSITION: Plant Manager
DATE WRITTEN:
REPORTS TO: Director of Operations
JOB SUMMARY and KEY OBJECTIVES
Directs and manages all plant operations with overall responsibilities for production, maintenance, quality, and other production-related activities.
KEY RESPONSIBILITIES and TASKS

- Directs and manages plant operations for production, maintenance, quality, and shipping and receiving.
- Coordinates plant activities through planning with departmental managers to insure that manufacturing objectives are accomplished in a timely and cost-effective manner.
- Develops and controls profits, plans, and budget.

- Implements cost effective systems of control over capital, operating expenditures, manpower, wages, and salaries.
- Manages CAM process.
- Establishes and monitors overall plant performance for production and quality standards.
- Controls and minimizes labor overtime, premium freight, and repair expenses.
- Maintains existing plant facilities and equipment; must replace or make adjustments to plant facilities and equipment when necessary.
- Provides leadership and training to accomplish the company goals and objectives.
- Implements and maintains preventive maintenance programs.
- Incorporates shop floor organization and plant cleanliness among plant personnel.
- Provides direction, development, and leadership to production supervisor.

PREFERRED QUALIFICATIONS and EDUCATION

- Bachelor's degree in related field or five years plant/general management experience in a manufacturing environment.
- Prior experience implementing ISO9001 in preparation for plant implementation.
- Experience managing in a union environment.
- Working knowledge of budgets and financial statements.
- Background with manufacturing methods, process improvement programs, and procedures required.

NOTE: The responsibilities and tasks outlined in this document are not exhaustive and may change as determined by the needs of the company.

In addition to this information about the job, you (as the manager) know that your company is disappointed that it has to look outside the company to fill this position, and has put a priority on developing existing staff to prepare them for future promotions. The company is also very concerned about rising costs and increased overtime.

With this knowledge and your job description in hand, it's time to research job postings. At Monster (www.monster.com), you type "Plant Manager" into the keyword search feature, and 1,000 plant manager references pop up. Browse through a few and see if anything sounds similar to your position.

1. How have other postings prioritized the job responsibilities?
2. Do you like the language they use in describing the position?
3. Can you differentiate your job from the others posted?

4. Has anyone emphasized employee development and cost control—issues that are very important to your company?

These postings are a mother lode of good information, and they should help you refine exactly what you want to put in the posting. Your job will be to keep from getting distracted and focus only on positions and descriptions that sound like your own.

With your initial research done, look back to your job description. How would you reorder the bullets in the description to prioritize what you really want? Remember that internal development and cost controls are important to your supervisors. Here is one way that you might prioritize the bullets to better reflect your company's needs:

JOB DESCRIPTION BULLETS	JOB POSTING BULLETS
Direct and manage plant operations for production, maintenance, quality, and shipping and receiving.	Direct and manage plant operations for production, maintenance, quality, and shipping and receiving.
Coordinate plant activities through planning with departmental managers to ensure the total manufacturing objectives are accomplished in a timely and cost-effective manner.	Provide leadership and training to accomplish company goals and objectives.
Develop and control profits, plans, and budget.	Implement cost-effective systems of control over capital, operating expenditures, manpower, wages, and salaries.
Implement cost-effective systems of control over capital, operating expenditures, manpower, wages, and salaries.	Control and minimize labor overtime, premium freight, and repair expenses.

2. Streamline Your Writing

Next, you want to hone your writing for space and impact. Short, punchy (and often grammatically incorrect) sentences are typically used to draw in the reader/candidate. Remember, you want to include as much information as possible, in the most interesting way. Here are some examples from our Plant Manager position:

JOB DESCRIPTION BULLETS	BRIEFER, PUNCHIER EXAMPLES
Control and minimize labor overtime, premium freight, and repair expenses.	Creatively manage overtime, freight, and repair costs to meet set goals.
Incorporates shop floor organization and plant cleanliness among plant personnel.	Provide leadership to team in the areas of plant organization and cleanliness.
Establish and monitor overall plant performance for production and quality standards.	Exceed established standards for production and quality.

In selling the job, you can use challenges (exceed established measures), appeal to people's desire for initiative (creatively manage), and choose words that people respond to positively (provide leadership as opposed to incorporate among plant personnel). By punching up your sentences, you can make your job posting look even more compelling to the right candidate.

Make it sound like fun. Action verbs are a great way to punch up your language and sell your job. By changing a few words here and there, you can make a job sound more interesting and more creative. For example, instead of implementing, try creating. Instead of meeting, try exceeding established goals. Don't manage; lead. Don't provide; design and implement. Don't coordinate plant activities; collaborate through cross-functional teams!

3. Remove Inside Information

Next, you want to strip that jargon out of your job description. Having worked at your company for a period of time, you may not even realize that your job posting contains words that might be meaningless to any outsider. In the sample job description above, the author has written, "Manages CAM process." This means little to the average person, but managing the capital asset maintenance process is critical to the job and should be spelled out.

And don't forget to take out any information that you don't want to make available to the public. Some companies peruse job postings to see what's interesting and important to their competitors. References to future products, strategies, or financials should all be removed before you post the job. For example, the sample description has a bullet that reads, "Experience implementing ISO9001 in preparation for plant implementation." This makes it clear to competitors not only that this plant has not yet implemented this important quality standard, but also that they need outside help in order to do so.

4. Describe Your Company

Include a short paragraph on the company itself, explaining what it does and why an applicant would want to work there. This is where you'll want to pitch what your company has to offer, without crossing the line into exaggeration or false promises.

> **EXAMPLE:** We are the industry leader in the manufacture of steel rule dies and complimentary tooling with facilities throughout the USA and an established global customer base. We offer excellent benefits, competitive salary plus bonus opportunity, 401(k), health, dental, life, prescription card. Pre-employment drug screening is required.

5. Next Steps

Close the description by letting applicants know what to do if they are interested in the position. Typically, you'll want to tell applicants whom to respond to, what materials to provide, and any deadlines for the application process.

> **EXAMPLE**
>
> **How to Apply:** Send a cover letter and resume to Human Resources, Nolo Press, 950 Parker Street, Berkeley, California, 94710, or email to jobs@nolo .com. Please include your name, address, telephone number, and email address (if applicable). We will contact you if we decide to pursue your application, but not otherwise. NO PHONE CALLS, PLEASE.

6. Putting It All Together

Below are a couple of examples of effective job postings. They describe and sell the position, while providing the information applicants need to evaluate the job and decide whether to apply.

EXAMPLE ONE:

Company X is seeking a Flash Game Developer to develop top quality game prototypes, games, and community features for our websites. The Flash Game Developer will work closely with game designers to create rapid prototypes of various game ideas. Additionally, this person will interface with other engineers, producers, artists, game designers, and musicians to create compelling, feature-rich games.

RESPONSIBILITIES:
- Brainstorm and create appealing game demonstrations and prototypes
- Create single-player and multiplayer Flash games from conception to launch
- Work with and help expand a flexible framework/SDK for use across many games

QUALIFICATIONS:
- Bachelor's degree in Computer Science or equivalent work experience
- Minimum 3–5 years experience in developing Flash games
- Advanced ActionScript 2.0 coding skills and strong familiarity with object-oriented principals
- Great game sense and knowledge of the game market
- Strong verbal and written communications skills
- Self-directed
- Must be organized, systematic, punctual, and goal-oriented

PLUSES:
- Art skills
- Solid understanding of how to optimize file sizes and performance
- Passion for games

Company X is a leading developer and publisher of online casual games for the mass market. The company offers free games, premium download games, and skill-based games through its websites www.CompanyX.com and www.sample.com. Company X also distributes its games through several leading Web properties and in 2004, Company X's top game, Behemoth™, was declared a Finalist for the 2004 Entertainment Awards as 'Downloadable Game of the Year.'

Qualified candidates should apply at www.CompanyX.com.

EXAMPLE TWO:

INVESTMENT CONSULTANT

Company Y is a leading global financial services firm. We provide investors with a broad range of brokerage, mutual fund, banking, and consumer financial products and services on an integrated basis.

We are currently seeking a licensed Investment Consultant for our Pocono Branch.

As an Investment Consultant at Company Y, you will assess, assist, and advise clients as they choose the services best suited for their needs. You will develop relationships with existing customers and build relationships with new customers. Your goal is to demonstrate to customers and prospects the value of the Company Y platform, resulting in asset accumulation and retention.

Typical daily activities include proactive, business development calls to prospects and customers; presentation of solutions to customers and prospects through face-to-face meetings; tracking your activities through our customer relationship management system; continuing to update your sales skills; and responding to leads generated through our supplemental business development efforts.

Our compensation philosophy reflects our deeply held belief that the customer relationship should come first and not be compromised by commission sales. Our Investment Consultants are paid a base salary and quarterly sales incentives based on individual production and Branch performance against both asset and new account targets. In addition, we offer a comprehensive benefits program that includes medical, dental, vision, and 401(k).

We have built a successful, customer-focused business model and an outstanding work environment. We value teamwork, integrity, service, open communication, and perseverance. If you want to work at a firm that truly values your contributions, consider a career at Company Y.

REQUIREMENTS:

Ideal candidates will have a Bachelor's degree; Series applicable license; 3 or more years of proactive, successful sales experience in the financial services industry. You must also be an outstanding communicator, possess comprehensive industry and investment knowledge, and have the ability to present complex financial solutions that allow customers to choose the right solutions for their needs.

QUALIFIED CANDIDATES SHOULD CONTACT:

Company Y

Attn: Sam Smythe, Branch Manager

100 Main Street, Suite 100

Big City, CA 90000

Fax: 800-555-1212

No phone calls please.

EOE M/F/D/V

This second example is a different style of writing—it includes full sentences rather than bullet points, and it uses a fair bit of financial lingo. It also does a great job of telling applicants about the company and why they might want to work there—and makes very clear that only customer-focused people need apply.

At the end of this chapter, you'll find a blank job posting template, which you can use to turn your job description into a posting that includes all of the information described above. (You'll also find a copy of the template in Appendix B and on the CD-ROM at the back of this book.)

B. Setting Pay Levels

Job descriptions are often used to help determine what to pay the position. Many of you have access to Human Resource departments to do the work of actually determining where the position falls on your company's organizational ladder, comparing it to the marketplace, and establishing a pay range. (For those of you who don't have an HR department to help, check out *The Manager's Legal Handbook*, by Lisa Guerin and Amy DelPo (Nolo), for tips on how to do this.)

Pay is typically based on an employee's skill set, background, and relative power within your organization. In other words, employees tend to make more money as they gain experience, skills, and responsibilities.

Each of these steps represents a new level of experience, skill, and/or responsibility—and each level should make more money than the previous level. Figuring out where a job falls on this scale will help you determine what the job should be paid. There are also other factors in determining pay, including your company's budget and what competitors pay for like positions.

Experience and Skill Set Increases

The job responsibilities listed in your job description will help determine where the position falls on this scale. While the title of the job serves as a clue (such as Manager versus Supervisor), larger companies often have more than one level of manager, with the pay increasing as the responsibilities grow.

Your Human Resources department (for those of you who have them) will be reading your job description very closely to try to place it within their compensation system. While you shouldn't write your description with a level (and/or pay range) in mind, it makes sense to know what kind of things are considered in determining pay. For example, check out the sample job level chart for administrative positions, below. You can see how the language used to describe job functions can help determine the level—and pay range—of the position. That's just one more reason why you should choose your words carefully when writing the description.

JOB LEVELS	FACTORS	KNOWLEDGE
1	Entry (Inexperienced)	Limited use and/or application of basic principles, theories, and concepts. Limited knowledge of industry practices and standards.
2	Intermediate (Experienced)	General application of concepts and principles. Frequent use and general knowledge of industry practices, techniques, and standards.
3	Senior (Career Level)	Complete understanding and application of principles, concepts, practices, and standards. Full knowledge of industry practices.
4	Specialist (Consultant to Mgmt.)	Contributes to the development of new concepts, techniques, and standards. Considered expert in field within the organization.
5	Senior Specialist (Consultant to Senior Mgmt.)	Develops advanced concepts, techniques, and standards. Develops new applications based on professional principles and theories. Viewed as expert in field within the corporation.

C. Conducting Interviews

Once you've written the job description, you have the litmus test for finding the right candidate to fill your job. Each bullet or concept contained in the job description represents an area for discussion in future interviews. How many times have you been interviewed and asked questions like these?

- Tell me about your biggest success.
- Tell me about your biggest failure.
- What are you most proud of?
- Pick a boss that you most admired and tell me why.
- Tell me about your background.

Questions like these are tried-and-true interview fillers. The interviewer can use them to figure out some of the applicant's strengths and weaknesses, as well as a bit about the applicant's values and work style. But they don't really help an interviewer figure out how well the applicant would do in the job at hand.

Now imagine that the interviewer has a prepared list of questions, prioritized in order of importance, such as:

- Give me an example of a time when you successfully cut your budget by a given percentage. How did you determine what to cut and what were the results of your actions?
- Inventory management is a critical part of this job. What size inventories have you managed, what processes did you use, and what were the results?

Questions like these provide the kind of detailed information you need to assess a candidate's qualifications. And you can create them right out of the information in your job description. The process is simple:

1. Take a bullet or statement from the Job Responsibilities section and determine the results of doing that task well.
2. Formulate an open-ended question to determine the candidate's abilities in that area.
3. Based on a few probable answers, create some follow-up questions to probe deeper into the candidate's experience and knowledge.
4. Write these questions down, and determine who on the interview team should cover each topic (if you are not the only interviewer).
5. Track how the different candidates answer these questions so you can compare and contrast their skills as you evaluate who would be best for the job.

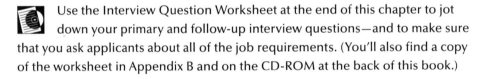 Use the Interview Question Worksheet at the end of this chapter to jot down your primary and follow-up interview questions—and to make sure that you ask applicants about all of the job requirements. (You'll also find a copy of the worksheet in Appendix B and on the CD-ROM at the back of this book.)

1. Coming Up With Questions

Your first step is to develop a list of questions, based on the specific skills and accomplishments you want from your new hire. Start by completing the exercise below:

EXERCISE 5:
DRAFT INTERVIEW QUESTIONS

Using a bullet from your job description, this exercise will help you develop an interview question and three follow-up questions that will help you figure out whether applicants can perform that function well.

1. Take a bullet or statement from the job functions section of your job description and determine the results of doing that task well.
2. Formulate an open-ended question to evaluate the candidate's abilities in that area.
3. Based on a few probable answers, create some follow-up questions to probe deeper into the candidate's experience and knowledge.

Job Function: _____

_____
_____
_____

Question _____

_____
_____
_____

Follow-up Question #1 _____

_____
_____
_____

Follow-up Question #2 _____

_____
_____
_____

Follow-up Question #3 _____

_____
_____
_____

The first step is to determine what a positive outcome of doing this task well would be. Increasing revenue would result in a higher commission check and increased revenues to the company. Formulate an open-ended question (a question that cannot be answered in one or two words) such as: "Tell me about a time when you beat your revenue numbers. How did you accomplish that?" If an applicant has no response, that tells you a lot right there. Most likely, your candidates will have an example to relate.

Follow-up questions could include things like "What process did you use to cultivate your customer base to achieve these numbers?" Because you're hiring for a management job, you might also want to ask "How did you motivate your team to achieve this?" Or, "How did you reward them?" You can also start interview questions with a leading statement, like this: "Your customers were critical in achieving your sales numbers. How did you work with them to make this happen?" While you don't want to ask too many leading questions, you do want to let your applicants know what kind of information you're looking for.

2. Conducting the Interview

When you have a strong list of questions, spend a moment thinking about who should ask them. Each person on the interview team has a different perspective or skill set, and someone else may be better qualified to judge the answers in a given area than you are. While it may be the toughest interview the applicant has experienced, you will have an incredible data set upon which to base your decision.

Take time during or immediately after the interview to write down your impressions of the candidates, including the answers that made an impact on you, whether positive or negative. This will be a great tool when you are comparing strong candidates against each other to decide whom to hire.

D. Orienting New Hires

In a perfect world, your new employee would walk in on the first day of work and make an immediate contribution to your team, proving to one and all what a great job you did during the hiring process. In the real world, however, your new employee will probably be dragged off immediately after walking in the door to attend a half-day orientation session that explains how to sign up for benefits, then returned to you in time for lunch. It becomes your job to make your new employee as productive as possible, as soon as possible. The job description that you wrote will really help you here, by making sure that you and your employee are on the same page, right from the start.

When you wrote the job description, you captured exactly what you expect from any employee doing that job. So, after you finish that first-day lunch with your new employee, pull out the description and go over it with him or her, to make sure your new hire knows what you expect and by when.

The process for this is simple:

- Set up time for an in-depth conversation with your new employee.
- Using the job description, prioritize what you would like done by when.
- Provide guidance on how best to achieve the goals you are laying out.
- Document your conversation so you can use it to measure progress.

This is an important conversation in your nascent relationship with your new employee. Of course, the interview and hiring process should have given the employee a good idea of what it will take to be successful in the position. Now you have the opportunity to clarify and prioritize your goals, and provide some guidance on how to achieve them.

1. Holding Your Orientation Meeting

The key to your success in using the job description as an orientation tool is to establish good communications with your new hire. On the very first day, when fear, uncertainty, and doubt will probably dominate your new employee's thoughts, set aside a good chunk of time to allay those concerns and provide a blueprint for the employee's first 90 days in the job. As you have doubtless experienced yourself, knowing what is expected of you lets you get off to a good start and allows you to contribute (and make an impact) much more quickly.

During your initial meeting, start by laying the ground rules for how you want to communicate. Let your employee know how much of your time he or she will have, how to get questions answered quickly, the best way to reach you, and so on. By setting a regular meeting time (often referred to as a 1:1 or status meeting), you can avoid daily interruptions, and give your employee confidence that he or she will have regular, scheduled interaction with you.

Once it's clear that you are there to support your employee, and you've agreed upon ways to keep each other up to date, it's time to establish priorities and set some timelines.

2. Build a Blueprint for the First 90 Days

There have been numerous studies done on how to improve productivity in the workforce. The consistent (but not surprising) conclusion of these studies is that giving a new employee a clear picture of what you expect increases productivity dramatically. And of course, if your employees are performing well, it reflects well on you as their manager.

Start prioritizing by looking at the job functions listed in the job description. List them in order of importance and add a time-line, so your employee will know exactly what he or she needs to accomplish. Typically, you'll want to create a short-term blueprint, so that you can monitor the employee's progress and step in early if you notice any problems.

For example, here's how the manager of this position would set up a 90-day blueprint:

JOB DESCRIPTION
Position Title: Receiving Manager
Basic Function:

A Receiving Manager is responsible for establishing and maintaining Guest Services, all the tasks involved with smooth daily operations of the Receiving Area and processing of store merchandise to the selling floor and/or stock room, all documentation related to that function, as well as the hiring and training of Early Morning Stocking (EMS) and Receiving Associates and their productivity.

Principal Responsibilities:

1. Ensures that each Guest receives outstanding Guest Service by providing a Guest-friendly environment which includes greeting and acknowledging every Guest, maintaining outstanding standards, solid product knowledge, and all other components of Guest Service.

2. Manages the receiving process (on site and off). Verifies all merchandise deliveries according to Company standards.

3. Recruits, trains, and develops Receiving associates, and cross trains Early Morning Stocking associates.

4. Supervises effectiveness and productivity of Receiving and EMS staff through continual communication and performance management; reacts to personnel performance issues.

5. Develops, and implements, manpower plans and executes recruitment strategies to fill staffing needs.

6. Supervises and assures the preparation of all merchandise for the selling floor, including verifying selling information through Purchase Orders and ticketing; ensures selling floor is appropriately stocked; complies with Company ticketing and signing guidelines.

7. Communicates advanced shipping information to Merchandise Managers.

8. Ensures timely and accurate input of all freight information through the Inventory Management System.

9. Ensures the accurate processing of all RTVs, charge sends, transfers, re-wraps, and salvage merchandise, including donations based on Company policies and procedures.

10. Ensures the proper receiving procedures are used for control of shortages. The general maintenance of the store; compliance with "Main Event" standards.

11. Assists in floor moves.

12. Any other duties as assigned by management.

Essential Physical Requirements:

(Lifting—Exactly how much, bending, climbing, driving equipment.)

1. Ability to process information and merchandise through computer system and POS register system.

2. Ability to communicate with associates and guests.

3. Ability to read, count, and write to accurately complete all documentation.

4. Ability to visually use all Purchase Codes and other shipping documentation.

5. Ability to freely access all areas of the store including selling floor, stock area, register area, and office.

6. Ability to operate and use all equipment necessary to manage a store.

7. Ability to climb ladders.

8. Ability to move and handle merchandise throughout the store generally weighing 0–75 pounds.

9. Ability to work varied hours/days to oversee store operations.

Austin, the store manager, has hired Sydney as her Receiving Manager. Syd's first day is tomorrow and Austin has let him know that he will be in Store Orientation from 9 a.m. until noon, followed by a welcome lunch. The afternoon will be spent with Austin herself, to provide Syd with a blueprint for success in his first 90 days, as well as to introduce him to the ways of the team that runs the store.

Austin, who has been managing people for years, prepares for her meeting with Sydney by using a simple worksheet to organize her thoughts. This worksheet will set the parameters for their conversation, then become documentation of what they both agree can be accomplished in the first 90 days. They will each get a copy at the end of the meeting, and refer to it during their weekly meetings.

90-DAY PLAN RECEIVING MANAGER			
Job Function	Short-Term Goal(s)	Resources Available	Time Due

Use the 90-Day Orientation Blueprint at the end of this chapter to create your own plan for new employees. (You'll also find a copy of the blueprint in Appendix B and on the CD-ROM at the back of this book.)

The Job Function column is taken directly from the job description. The Short-Term Goal is created by setting a measurement for the job function—what can feasibly be accomplished by a new employee in the first three months. Resources Available is a cheat sheet for Austin's new employees to let them know what help they will have in achieving their goals. And the Time Due is a mutually agreed-upon date for finishing the short-term goal. With this worksheet, Austin can now take the functions of the job description, turn them into goals, and communicate them to Sydney.

Austin knows that a few items are critical in the short term: the receiving function has two open positions that must be staffed quickly. The company is also having a problem with lost shipments, which must be addressed. And the whole receiving team needs some training, focused on making them successful in the future. With those priorities firmly in mind, Austin fleshes out the worksheet as follows:

90-DAY PLAN
Receiving Manager
Start Date: July 1

JOB FUNCTION: Develop and implement manpower plans and execute recruitment strategies to fill staffing needs.

SHORT-TERM GOAL(S)	RESOURCES AVAILABLE	TIME DUE
Create accurate manpower plan within constraints of budget	Prior year's manpower plan, current year's budget, template from Finance (Attached)	Sept. 1
Write job descriptions for two open positions	Nolo's Job Description Handbook (Company Library)	July 15
Post jobs on Hot Jobs and Monster	Human Resources (ext. 51155)	July 22
Set interview team	HR and Austin	July 22
Complete interview process	Interview team	August 15
Fill both open positions	Store's Hiring Standards document (Attached)	Sept. 15

JOB FUNCTION: Manages the receiving process (on site and off). Verifies all merchandise deliveries according to Company standards.

SHORT-TERM GOAL(S)	RESOURCES AVAILABLE	TIME DUE
Familiarize yourself with Company Standards for receiving	Standards Policy Manual (www.policies.com/receiving)	July 22
Analyze existing processes to identify receiving errors	Sample Process analysis (attached)	August 15
Develope written plan to address lost shipments	Sample Plan (attached), Austin	August 30
Implement plan and reduce loss by 75%	Staff	Sept. 30

JOB FUNCTION: Supervises effectiveness and productivity of Receiving and EMS staff through continual communication and performance management; reacts to personnel performance issues.		
SHORT-TERM GOAL(S)	**RESOURCES AVAILABLE**	**TIME DUE**
Meet with team as group and in 1:1 meetings	Calendar software	July 7
Set individual and departmental goals and communicate to each	Sample goal sheet, Austin	August 15
Schedule Team Building exercise	Human Resources, Austin	Sept. 15
Communicate and address any personnel issues discovered	Store's Progressive Discipline policy (www.policies.com)	Sept. 30

Sydney certainly has his work cut out for him! Remember, Austin is setting the actual dates for completion in the orientation meeting itself, which allows Sydney to give some input on when he thinks he can accomplish this list. By creating this blueprint, both Sydney and Austin are crystal clear on what is expected, and Sydney has the resources available to complete the work.

3. Modify and Update the 90-Day Blueprint

Just as job descriptions are living documents that require on-going care, the 90-day blueprint may need to be updated as well. For example, it might not be possible for Sydney to hire two new employees in just a few months, for reasons completely outside of his control. During his weekly meeting with Austin, Sydney can explain any roadblocks he has encountered in meeting these dates. Together, Sydney and Austin can decide whether to allow more time, change directions, or even reprioritize Sydney's goals.

E. Measuring and Managing Performance

Evaluating employee performance is often the most challenging part of a manager's job. It can be tremendously complicated if you have to struggle with legal issues, interpersonal tensions, accusations of favoritism or discrimination, or problem employees. And, if you manage more than a few employees, it can be tough to remember how someone performed throughout the year when it's time to do a formal, annual performance appraisal.

So how do you avoid these issues, to the extent possible? By giving your employees relevant feedback in a timely fashion. Of course, every company has its own methods and forms for measuring performance. (If your company hasn't come up with an effective performance appraisal tool, check out *The Performance Appraisal Handbook*, by Amy DelPo (Nolo)—it explains how to measure and manage performance, and provides a system of feedback and documentation that is both effective and easy to use.) But no matter what system you use, the key to successful performance management is letting your employees know how they are doing.

Your skills and abilities as a manager will be measured by how your team performs. Getting the maximum output from well-qualified, engaged employees is the most basic definition of good management. And the best way to become a good manager is to let your employees know exactly what you want them to accomplish, then meet with them regularly to make sure they are making progress (and provide any assistance they might need).

Although it should go without saying, employees need to know what you expect of them in order to meet those expectations. Human Resource professionals have numerous war stories about how miscommunication caused serious trouble. Here's an example:

EXAMPLE: Laura was the customer service manager for a communications company. She managed ten people, whose jobs ranged from customer service representative to commissions analyst. Laura's department was at its most busy during the crunch time at the close of a quarter, when they were re-sponsible for making sure that all open orders were shipped before the quar-ter closed, so they could be counted as revenue for the company. They would often work until the early morning hours during the final week of the quarter.

It was during one of these early mornings that Laura received a call from her manager, Stephanie. Stephanie told Laura that unless they could find an-other $100,000 in shipments, the company would miss their numbers for the quarter. Could Laura please do everything she could to find and ship those extra orders? Laura said absolutely, and began to comb the future shipment logs. Here was an order to be shipped the week after the quarter closed! If Laura just moved that date up, they could recognize the revenue, and make their numbers. She changed the ship date and notified her team to ship the product.

Three weeks later, as the finance department was closing the books on the quarter, they could not find a request from that customer to move the ship date. Stephanie went to Laura and asked about the documentation. Lau-ra told Stephanie there was no documentation—she just moved the date up on her own in order to help the company meet its numbers. Stephanie had no choice but to write Laura up on a final written warning, and many in the company believed Laura should be fired. Stephanie realized her role in the miscommunication, and Laura's job was safe … this time.

Good communication is hard work—it takes focus and discipline. You'll have to check in often and keep track of what you and your employees agree upon. And that's where the job description comes in: You can use it as a performance baseline, to make sure that you and your employee are on the same page, using the same methods to measure performance. This simple exercise will go a long way toward eliminating confusion and misinterpretation—either of which can lead to more serious problems down the road.

Chapter 1 explained a simple method to convert a job description into a performance measurement tool, simply by adding a rating column next to each function. Because you took the time to write a comprehensive description, you have already done a lot of the work of setting up a performance management system. You can use this simple tool weekly, monthly, or as a finishing touch on your 90-day plan for your new employee. Keep copies of this informal performance feedback to help you build the documentation necessary to either reward (promote or give a bonus to) or discipline your employee.

Get some legal help. Many managers try to avoid any unnecessary contact with their legal department—after all, lawyers often want managers to spend more time documenting and providing proof that their decisions were correct, which leaves less time for you to do your job. But there's a good reason for this vigilance: incomplete, inaccurate, or nonexistent paperwork can torpedo your company's chances of successfully defending itself in an employment lawsuit. While you don't want to spend too much time documenting every conversation and interaction with your employees, it makes good sense to talk to your legal or HR department to make sure that you're on the right track when giving performance feedback.

Test Your Knowledge

Questions

1. Job descriptions are mostly useful during the hiring process.

   A. True   B. False

2. Here are some of the steps you should follow in creating a job posting. Put them in the proper order:

   A. Describe your company   B. Streamline your prose

   C. Explain how to apply   D. Prioritize the job functions

3. When working to streamline your prose, it is important to make sure that your language is flowery and interesting.

   A. True   B. False

4. Using industry jargon in your job description will help ensure that you attract only applicants who know the field.

   A. True   B. False

5. Job descriptions should include the salary for the position.

   A. True   B. False

6. You should use the job description to come up with interview questions.

   A. True   B. False

7. Which of the following is not a step in creating an effective orientation for your new employee(s)?

   A. Set up time for an in-depth conversation with your new hire

   B. Using the job description, build a 90-day blueprint for their first few months on the job

   C. Modify the job description based on what the new employee wants to do

   D. Provide guidance on how to best achieve the goals you are laying out

Answers

1. **False.** Although job descriptions certainly can be used in hiring, they are also useful in every other phase of the employment relationship.

2. **D, B, A, and C.** Prioritize first, streamline your prose, describe your company, and close by explaining how to apply.

3. **False.** Streamlining your prose means making it as interesting as possible in the simplest, clearest way.

4. **False.** Unless you are certain that the words or acronyms you are using are widely understood in your field, you should leave them out.

5. **False.** It's better to leave salary information out of the description.

6. **True.** The job description is a great starting point for planning your interview.

7. **C.** You will very rarely need to modify a job description in the orientation process. While all the functions on the job description may not be of the highest priority, they will most likely come into play later in the life cycle of the job.

YOUR COMPANY
JOB POSTING

Job title:

Location:

JOB SUMMARY

ESSENTIAL FUNCTIONS

JOB REQUIREMENTS AND QUALIFICATIONS

ABOUT OUR COMPANY

HOW TO APPLY

YOUR COMPANY

INTERVIEW QUESTION WORKSHEET

Job title:

Location:

Candidate's Name: Date of Interview:

JOB SUMMARY

ESSENTIAL FUNCTIONS

Function Number One:

Question 1:

- Potential Follow-up question:

- Potential Follow-up question:

Function Number Two:

Question 2:

- Potential Follow-up question:

- Potential Follow-up question:

Function Number Three:

Question 3:

- Potential Follow-up question:

- Potential Follow-up question:

Function Number Four:

Question 4:

- Potential Follow-up question:

- Potential Follow-up question:

Function Number Five:

Question 5:

- Potential Follow-up question:

- Potential Follow-up question:

JOB REQUIREMENTS AND QUALIFICATIONS

Does the candidate fulfill your educational requirements (or have equivalent experience)?

Has the candidate fulfilled the training requirements (licenses, programs, or certificates)?

Does the candidate have the specific experience necessary to do the job?

OTHER INFORMATION

Can the candidate meet the other requirements of the job?

- Travel issues

- Work hours

- On-call requirements

- Other

YOUR COMPANY

90-DAY ORIENTATION BLUEPRINT

Employee's Name: Start Date:

Job Title: 90-Day End Date:

JOB SUMMARY

PRIMARY FUNCTIONS AND DELIVERABLES

Job Function	Short-Term Goal(s)	Resources Available	Time Due

COMMENTS AND EXPECTATIONS AT BEGINNING OF PERIOD

COMMENTS AND RESULTS AT END OF 90 DAYS

Job Function	Short-Term Goal(s)	Results	Comments

Chapter 6

Troubleshooting

I f you've carefully followed the process outlined in this book, you should now be the proud owner of an accurate, compelling job description, a document that will help you with your most important managerial tasks while keeping you out of legal trouble. But even if you draft, revise, and polish a stellar job description, you might run into problems when you take it for a test drive in the real world. What if the position for which you've written a description could better be done by another department, or by an existing employee? What if you have to add new job duties to keep up with changes at your company? What if your existing employees believe the new position is a threat to their responsibilities or authority?

This chapter will help you deal with these issues, and a few other problems that you might have to handle as you put your job descriptions to work.

A. Deciding Whether to Hire

The process of writing a job description requires you to look closely at your organization and your team. This is a good thing! It allows you to step back and consider what you—and your company—really need. But what should you do if you aren't sure, after you've brainstormed and crafted the essential functions of the position, whether the duties you've identified really justify hiring a new employee? Here are some issues to consider:

- **Can you divide these job functions among your existing staff without putting too much stress on the system?** If so, introduce the idea to your team, and promise to revisit how things are going in a relatively short time frame. Assure them that after 30 days, you'll check back in to see whether things are working out—and make changes if they are not. If your reports know that they have an escape route, it will help offset any resistance they might feel.

- **Are these functions critical enough to require immediate hiring?** Your first impulse will probably be to answer with a resounding "yes!" But before you move on, make sure your reaction makes sense—and isn't based simply on fear or routine. If someone has left a position, it's almost an automatic response to try to fill it as quickly as possible. Yet life goes on while the position is empty. Pay attention to the amount of anxiety your team feels while that job is empty. If stress levels are high, it's probably a good idea to fill the job. If no one notices the empty chair, you may not have an urgent need to fill the position.

- **Could any of the functions of this job provide a real growth opportunity for a current employee?** By spreading around some of the work, even if it's in an "acting" role, you will get a chance not only to motivate your staff to take on new challenges, but also to see how they perform at a different level. You can always fill the position later if it doesn't work out.

If you conclude that these job functions are vital and cannot be done by your existing employees, yet you still aren't sure that they add up to a full-time position, consider accomplishing these tasks a different way. Here are a couple of options:

- **Create a part-time position.** By hiring someone for a limited number of hours, you might be able to get the work done in a more cost-efficient way for the company. You'll also have access to a pool of job applicants that are unable (or unwilling) to consider a full-time position, including working parents, those attending school, or people who have retired from the full-time workforce, but still want to stay active in their field.

- **Hire an independent contractor.** This is a great option for certain types of work—typically, special projects that have a limited time frame and are beyond your current team's expertise. For example, you might consider bringing in a contractor to design a website, establish financial systems and controls for your bookkeeping department, or do the public relations work for a new product launch. However, government agencies take a very close look at workers whom companies hire as independent contractors. Because many companies have wrongly called workers "independent contractors" just to avoid payroll tax obligations and other legal duties, the IRS and other agencies will want to make sure that contractors really are running their own independent businesses and offering services in a limited capacity to your company. But that's not all there is to it: The IRS uses a 20-factor test to decide how workers should be classified (check it out at www.wwwebtax. com/general/independent_contractor.htm), and other agencies use different tests. This doesn't mean you should avoid categorizing workers as independent contractors, but you'll want to make sure that you're well within the rules. For help, take a look at *Working With Independent Contractors*, by Stephen Fishman (Nolo).

B. Moving the Position to Another Department

Unless you work in human resources and writing job descriptions for the entire company is, well, part of your job description, you are probably writing a description for a position within your own part of the organization. But as an enlightened manager with an eye toward overall corporate success, step back and think about this again. Would another group or team be better served by having this skill set and functional responsibility in their organization? Would your group be more productive at its own work if these responsibilities and functions were in a different group? Would it be better for your company to give this position to another department?

> **EXAMPLE:** Laurie manages a staff of eight in the recruiting department. She has overall responsibility for filling all of the positions within her company. To speed up the hiring process, Laurie hired a compensation expert reporting to her, to help her decide what to offer candidates and determine starting salaries, among other things.
>
> Last week, Laurie's expert quit without notice. Laurie quickly picked up this book and began brainstorming all of the functions that this person had handled. She came up with a list of factors that she thought were necessary to be successful in the job and developed a number of essential functions. She vetted her rough draft against the potential legal pitfalls and scrubbed it for clarity and tone. That done, Laurie went about posting the job.
>
> Later that day, as she thought about her quick action, Laurie realized that the functions that she had so carefully described really belonged in the company's compensation department. That group was better suited to select the right person for the job. She also knew deep down that this talent could be useful to others in the company, beyond her department. Although it meant she would have to work more closely with a group outside of her own organization, Laurie decided to offer the position to the compensation department—with the caveat that their new employee must prioritize the recruiters' needs first.

Your first impulse as a manager is typically to protect your resources and keep your team intact. But by considering the overall needs of the organization, you may be able to better serve it by making some changes. You can also allow your team to focus on their primary duties. In the example above, Laurie's team is now made up purely of recruiters, and they can focus solely on filling the empty positions in the company. Additionally, the compensation expert is now in an organization where career mobility can occur, offering the chance for promotions and new challenges.

C. If the Job Changes Over Time

If the job functions change, then the job description should change. The job description that you write when you're planning to hire someone may not describe exactly the same job that you eventually fill—or the job that employee is doing a year later. Companies, departments, and teams change, as do business priorities and technologies. There are plenty of good reasons why you might decide, after writing a description, to divide job duties differently, turn one position into two, or hire someone with a different (but equally valuable) skill set. And sometimes, an employee will take on new responsibilities or drop some tasks that weren't working out. Obviously, you shouldn't ignore these changes and opportunities by adhering rigidly to your old job description. Instead, you should update the description to reflect the actual job.

Although a job description can benefit you and your company in lots of ways, it could actually work against you if you don't keep it up to date. For example, you can't successfully manage performance using an outdated description that doesn't list the true functions of the job. Your hiring process will certainly suffer if you base your posting and interview questions on an obsolete position description. And an outdated job description could cause legal problems as well.

You should update a job description if:

- you add or delete a function from the job
- you hire someone with a unique skill set that doesn't quite track the old description
- you need a higher level of contribution from that position, such as a new skill or body of knowledge, or
- the requirements of the job change (for example, a specific certificate or license is now necessary to do the job).

This is not an exhaustive list of reasons to change your job description. A good rule of thumb is to review the job description with your employee on a regular basis to make certain that it still reflects the work the employee is doing. What constitutes a regular basis will vary from situation to situation. In a well-established company, perhaps once a year is enough. In a fast moving, dynamic company, quarterly might be a better time frame. Ad hoc updates may also be in order. Don't wait for a regular review period; update the job description as you go.

If someone is currently doing the job you are describing, make sure to get his or her input about the accuracy of the job description. You probably don't need to have your employee sign the new description, but at least note in your calendar when he or she reviewed it. If you both agree about the nature of the job, it could mitigate any conflict that might arise from poor performance or management issues.

D. Adding New Job Functions After an Employee Starts Work

Section C, above, explains how to update a job description if the job has changed over time. But what if the job hasn't changed yet—but you want it to? Are your hands tied because the job description doesn't include the new functions you want to add?

No. Don't let the job description hamstring you in handing out new duties. While you made every attempt to accurately depict the job, things in business change, often very quickly. This is why you took great care not to make any promises in the description—and it's why many companies include a disclaimer in their descriptions, stating that descriptions are not contracts and that job functions are subject to change at the company's discretion. The job description is a living document, one that you are entitled to change if you wish (always make sure your employees have the most current version).

Don't forget to communicate these changes in a positive light. Tell your employee why new responsibilities are being assigned—especially if you are giving more work to an employee who has proved able to handle it. Explain the importance of the new duties and how long they will last (if applicable). Make sure the employee feels capable of handling these new duties. Help set priorities so that you are both clear about responsibilities and deadlines.

E. Handling Coworker Concerns

Sometimes, your group will be overjoyed to hear that a new position has been created—it's one more set of hands to do the work. Other times, however, current employees might feel territorial, concerned that the new position will take away some of their responsibility or authority.

This can be an issue in companies of all sizes. Small businesses have the advantage of instilling feelings of ownership amongst the whole team. Everyone pulls together to be successful, and each relies on the other much like the members of a sports team. Change of any kind can feel threatening in this type of environment. Involving your employees in the process can alleviate these fears. Ask your employees to review a draft of your job description. If you are hiring in response to a change in your business, share that change to the extent that you can. Explain why the change is necessary, and what it means to the people working for you. Work to assure them that hiring this new person will benefit the team as a whole.

In larger companies, competition for advancement can get fierce. Something as simple as adding a resource to relieve someone who has too much work can still worry the very person you thought you were helping! You can take care of these issues much as you would in a smaller company, by

- communicating your intent early and often
- involving your employees in the process, to the extent possible, and
- checking in regularly to make sure that everyone feels comfortable going forward.

Things can be more complicated if you are hiring for a project that has not yet been announced. One of your employees might discover your job posting and, not knowing the whole story, sound the alarm at the water cooler. Expect that anytime you post a job, even "confidentially," your staff will hear about it. A recruiter might even cold call your own employee about a confidential position opening in your own department!

This type of situation is bound to be a bit sticky. Your staff must not have been qualified (or perhaps available) to take this new assignment, or you wouldn't have had to look outside of the company. But now you have a disgruntled team, sure that you are not sharing the whole truth with them. The best advice here is to own up to the fact that there is something confidential going on, and assure them that you will let them in on the details by a particular date (hopefully in advance of your new person's first day). Although this won't necessarily alleviate everyone's anxiety, it will at least take the mystery out of the situation, and allow your team to refocus on the work in front of them.

F. Employees and Applicants With Disabilities

As explained in Chapter 2, the purpose of delineating the essential functions of a position is to clarify your obligations toward applicants and employees with disabilities. If a function is truly essential, then an employee who cannot perform it, with or without a reasonable accommodation, is not qualified for the job. However, an employee who can perform all of a position's essential functions is qualified, even if that person requires a reasonable accommodation to do the work. And if you designate certain functions as "nonessential" in your job description, you cannot refuse to hire a disabled applicant solely because of his or her inability to do one of these tasks.

So far, so good. But what happens when someone with a disability actually applies for a position? In these situations, you will need to know exactly what the Americans with Disabilities Act (ADA), the law that protects people with disabilities from job discrimination, requires. (See Chapter 2 for more information on the ADA, including which companies must comply with it.) This section provides a brief overview of the ADA's requirements in this area; for more information, see *Federal Employment Laws*, by Lisa Guerin and Amy DelPo (Nolo).

You will undoubtedly want to make sure that any applicant you consider hiring can do the job. But the ADA protects applicants from discrimination—and from intrusive questioning about disabilities. For example, it is not legal to ask whether an applicant has ever had a disability, suffered from a particular disease, been hospitalized, or seen a psychiatrist. On the other hand, you are well within your rights to ask whether an applicant can perform all of the essential functions of a job, and how he or she would do so. This is where your job description will come in very handy: You can hand the applicant a complete list of essential functions, then ask how the applicant plans to perform each one. This will also give applicants a chance to let you know whether they need a reasonable accommodation to do the job. (Unless an applicant tells you of his or her disability or the disability is obvious, however, you may not ask whether the applicant will require a reasonable accommodation to do the job.)

If an applicant does require a reasonable accommodation, you will need to know exactly what you are—and are not—obligated to provide. Accommodating a worker means providing assistance or making changes to the job or workplace that will enable the worker to do the job. For example, a worker with attention deficit disorder might need a quiet, distraction-free workspace, while a worker in a wheelchair may need a lower desktop.

However, not every accommodation is considered "reasonable" in the eyes of the law. Employers do not have to provide an accommodation if it would cause their business "undue hardship." Whether an accommodation creates an undue hardship depends on a number of factors, including:

- the cost of the accommodation
- the size and financial resources of your business
- the structure of your business, and
- the effect the accommodation would have on your business.

Want more information on the ADA and reasonable accommodation?
Check out the website of the Equal Employment Opportunity Commission at www.eeoc.gov. You can download a number of factsheets, questions and answers on reasonable accommodation, and other resources. The website of the Job Accommodation Network (JAN), at www.jan.wvu.edu, provides information, consulting services, links to other sites that deal with disability issues, and much more.

An applicant may also need a reasonable accommodation to complete your application process. For example, if you give a written test to applicants for a sales position to test their knowledge of various sales techniques, you might offer to read the test to a blind applicant. This accommodation makes sense because sight is not required for the job—but it is required for the test. However, you don't have to provide an accommodation if the skills the test requires are necessary for the job. For example, if you were hiring an airline pilot, that person would have to be able to see to do the job well, so there would be no need to come up with a test that doesn't screen out blind applicants.

Test Your Knowledge

Questions

1. A carefully written job description will always result in a high- quality hire

   A. True   B. False

2. If one of your employees quits without notice, you should immediately:

   A. Post the job and begin the hiring process

   B. Promote one of your other employees into that position

   C. Farm out the work to the rest of team for 30 days to see how they like it

   D. Spend a little time describing and designing the job to see which method of getting the work done makes the most sense

3. Which of the following is probably not a good way to fill a job opening?

   A. Hire a full-time person   B. Hire an independent contractor

   C. Give the work to your best performer   D. Bring on a part-time employee

4. If a person leaves your department, you should immediately update the job description and start the hiring process.

   A. True   B. False

5. A carefully worded, well-written job description will last a lifetime.

   A. True   B. False

6. If you update a job description, you should give a copy to the person who is currently doing the job.

   A. True   B. False

7. Job descriptions should:

   A. Remain confidential until the hire is made

   B. Be shared amongst your team as soon as you have completed them

   C. Be shared in a manner that best fits your work situation

   D. Be posted in a central place, accessible to all

8. The legal purpose of listing essential job functions is to:

   A. Prioritize what is most important in a job

   B. Clarify your obligations toward applicants and employees with disabilities

   C. Show applicants which functions are nonnegotiable

Answers

1. **False.** A carefully written job description may result in a good hire, but it may also highlight another way of getting the work done, by temporary help, part-time workers, or your existing team.

2. **D.** Spend a little time describing and designing the job to see which method of getting the work done makes the most sense. While your first impulse may be to fill the gap as quickly as possible, you will save yourself time (and potentially money) in the long run if you consider your options first.

3. **C.** Give all the work to your best performer. Although it is tempting to give more responsibility to your top performer, you don't want to overburden that person. Spend some time with your employee to find out whether any responsibilities in the open position might be a good fit, but don't just pile the whole position onto your star's shoulders.

4. **False.** As a good manager, you should always consider the possibility that this job may belong in a different department where it might be a better fit.

5. **False.** A job description is a living document that will change with the vagaries of the business and the growth of the person doing the job. Set a regular update period to look at the job description and make sure that it still accurately reflects the work that is being done. If a new duty or function is added, that will require an update as well.

6. **True.** The job description is a great tool to set expectations for your employees. If your expectations change such that they warrant an update to the description, your employee should know that.

7. **C.** Be shared in a manner that best fits your situation. Stay sensitive to the fact that your team will want to know your plans, and that it is highly likely that a confidential hire will not remain confidential for long. Keep your team in the loop to the extent that you can, or promise them a date by which you can explain all.

8. **B.** Clarify your obligations toward applicants and employees with disabilities. Essential functions are those which are critical to the job, and the inability to perform them without reasonable accommodation could result in a candidate not being qualified for the job. ∎

Appendix A

How to Use the CD-ROM

The tools and checklists in Appendix B as well as a PowerPoint presentation based on this book are included on a CD-ROM in the back of the book. This CD-ROM, which can be used with Windows computers, installs files that you use with software programs that are already installed on your computer. It is not a stand-alone software program. Please read this appendix and the README.TXT file included on the CD-ROM for instructions on using the Forms CD.

Note to Mac users: This CD-ROM and its files should also work on Macintosh computers. Please note, however, that Nolo cannot provide technical support for non-Windows users.

How to View the README File

If you do not know how to view the file README.TXT, insert the Forms CD-ROM into your computer's CD-ROM drive and follow these instructions:

- **Windows 98, 2000, Me, and XP:** (1) On your PC's desktop, double click the My Computer icon; (2) double click the icon for the CD-ROM drive into which the Forms CD-ROM was inserted; (3) double click the file README.TXT.
- **Macintosh:** (1) On your Mac desktop, double click the icon for the CD-ROM that you inserted; (2) double click on the file README.TXT.

While the README file is open, print it out by using the Print command in the File menu.

Two different kinds of forms are contained on the CD-ROM:

- Word processing (RTF) files that you can open, complete, print, and save with your word processing program (see Section B, below), and
- A PowerPoint presentation (PPS) that can be viewed with Microsoft Power-Point Viewer (see Section C, below).

See Section D, below, for a list of files and and their file formats.

A. Installing the Files Onto Your Computer

Before you can do anything with the files on the CD-ROM, you need to install them onto your hard disk. In accordance with U.S. copyright laws, remember that copies of the CD-ROM and its files are for your personal use only.

Insert the Forms CD and do the following:

1. Windows 98, 2000, Me, and XP Users

Follow the instructions that appear on the screen. (If nothing happens when you insert the Forms CD-ROM, then (1) double click the My Computer icon; (2) double click the icon for the CD-ROM drive into which the Forms CD-ROM was inserted; and (3) double click the file WELCOME.EXE.)

By default, all the files are installed to the \Job Description Resources folder in the \Program Files folder of your computer. A folder called "Job Description Resources" is added to the "Programs" folder of the Start menu.

2. Macintosh Users

Step 1: If the "Job Description CD" window is not open, open it by double clicking the "Job Description CD" icon.

Step 2: Select the "Job Description Resources" folder icon.

Step 3: Drag and drop the folder icon onto the icon of your hard disk.

B. Using the Word Processing Files

This section concerns the files that can be opened and edited with your word processing program.

All word processing forms come in rich text format. These files have the extension ".RTF." For example, the file for Exercise 1: Brainstorm Work Traits discussed in Chapter 3 is on the file Exercise1.rtf. All forms, their file names, and file formats are listed in Section D, below.

RTF files can be read by most recent word processing programs including all versions of MS Word for Windows and Macintosh, WordPad for Windows, and recent versions of WordPerfect for Windows and Macintosh.

To use an RTF file from the CD you must: (1) open the file in your word processor or text editor; (2) edit the file by filling in the required information; (3) print it out; (4) rename and save your revised file.

The following are general instructions. However, each word processor uses different commands to open, format, save, and print documents. Please read your word processor's manual for specific instructions on performing these tasks.

Do not call Nolo's technical support if you have questions on how to use your word processor.

Step 1: Opening a File

There are three ways to open the word processing files included on the CD-ROM after you have installed them onto your computer.

- Windows users can open a file by selecting its "shortcut" as follows: (1) Click the Windows "Start" button; (2) open the "Programs" folder; (3) open the "Job Description Resources" subfolder; and (4) click on the shortcut to the form you want to work with.

- Both Windows and Macintosh users can open a file directly by double clicking on it. Use My Computer or Windows Explorer (Windows 98, 2000, Me, or XP) or the Finder (Macintosh) to go to the folder you installed or copied the CD-ROM's files to. Then, double click on the specific file you want to open.

- You can also open a file from within your word processor. To do this, you must first start your word processor. Then, go to the File menu and choose the Open command. This opens a dialog box where you will tell the program (1) the type of file you want to open (*.RTF); and (2) the location and name of the file (you will need to navigate through the directory tree to get to the folder on your hard disk where the CD's files have been installed). If these directions are unclear you will need to look through the manual for your word processing program—Nolo's technical support department will not be able to help you with the use of your word processing program.

Where Are the Files Installed?

Windows Users
- RTF files are installed by default to a folder named \Job Description Resources in the \Program Files folder of your computer.

Macintosh Users
- RTF files are located in the "Job Description Resources" folder.

Step 2: Editing Your Document

Fill in the appropriate information according to the instructions and samples in the book. Underlines are used to indicate where you need to enter your information. Be sure to delete the underlines from your edited document. If you do not know how to use your word processor to edit a document, you will need to look through the manual for your word processing program—Nolo's technical support department will not be able to help you with the use of your word processing program.

Step 3: Printing Out the Document

Use your word processor's or text editor's "Print" command to print out your document. If you do not know how to use your word processor to print a document, you will need to look through the manual for your word processing program—Nolo's technical support department will not be able to help you with the use of your word processing program.

Step 4: Saving Your Document

After completing your document, use the "Save As" command to save and rename the file. Because all the files are "read-only" you will not be able to use the "Save" command. This is for your protection. If you save the file without renaming it, the underlines that indicate where you need to enter your information will be lost and you will not be able to create a new document with this file without recopying the original file from the CD-ROM.

If you do not know how to use your word processor to save a document, you will need to look through the manual for your word processing program—Nolo's technical support department will not be able to help you with the use of your word processing program.

C. Using the PowerPoint Presentation

"Writing Great Job Descriptions," a presentation intended for use in staff training, is included on the CD-ROM in Microsoft's PowerPoint Show (PPS) format. You must have the Microsoft PowerPoint or PowerPoint Viewer installed on your computer to use this file. PowerPoint Viewer is available for Windows and Macintosh systems. If you don't already have this software, you can download a free copy of PowerPoint Viewer at www.microsoft.com/downloads.

All files and their file formats are listed in Section D, below.

Step 1: Opening the Presentation

The PowerPoint presentation, like the word processing files, can be opened one of three ways.

- Windows users can open a file by selecting its "shortcut" as follows: (1) Click the Windows "Start" button; (2) open the "Programs" folder; (3) open the "Job Description Resources" subfolder; and (4) click on the shortcut to "Writing Great Job Descriptions."
- Both Windows and Macintosh users can open a file directly by double clicking on it. Use My Computer or Windows Explorer (Windows 98, 2000, Me, or XP) or the Finder (Macintosh) to go to the folder you created and copied the CD-ROM's files to. Then, double click on the specific file you want to open.
- You can also open a PPS file from within PowerPoint or PowerPoint Viewer. To do this, you must first start PowerPoint or PowerPoint Viewer. Then, go to the File menu and choose the Open command. This opens a dialog box where you will tell the program the location and name of the file (you will need to navigate through the directory tree to get to the folder on your hard disk where the CD's files have been installed). If these directions are unclear you will need to look through the program's help—Nolo's technical support department will not be able to help you with the use of PowerPoint or PowerPoint Viewer.

Where Is the PowerPoint File Installed?

- **Windows Users:** the PowerPoint file is installed by default to a folder named \Job Description Resources in the \Program Files folder of your computer.
- **Macintosh Users:** the PowerPoint file is located in the "Job Description Resources" folder.

Step 2: Viewing the Presentation

To progress through the presentation, simply left click anywhere on the screen. To return to a previous screen or the beginning of the presentation, or to end the presentation, right click and select the appropriate option from the drop down menu.

D. Files Provided on the Forms CD-ROM

The following files are included in rich text format (RTF):

FILE NAME	FORM TITLE
Exercise1.rtf	Exercise 1: Brainstorm Work Traits
Exercise2.rtf	Exercise 2: Brainstorm Job Functions
Exercise3.rtf	Exercise 3: Prioritize Job Functions
Exercise4.rtf	Exercise 4: Create Compelling Bullet Points
Exercise5.rtf	Exercise 5: Draft Interview Questions
JobWorksheet.rtf	Job Description Worksheet
JobTemplate.rtf	Job Description Template
GoldenRules.rtf	Golden Rules Checklist
LegalIssues.rtf	Legal Issues Checklist
JobPosting.rtf	Job Posting Template
InterviewWorksheet.rtf	Interview Question Worksheet
Orientation.rtf	90-Day Orientation Blueprint
ForTrainers.rtf	PowerPoint Instructions for Trainers

The following file is included in Power Point Show format (PPS):

FILE NAME	FORM TITLE
Training.pps	Writing Great Job Descriptions

Appendix B

Tools and Checklists

EXERCISE 1: BRAINSTORM WORK TRAITS

This exercise will help you figure out which work traits you want to attract—and which you want to avoid—through your job description.

1. On the chart below, quickly write five positive traits—things that you like to see in your employees—on the plus side, and five negative traits on the minus side. It may help to think about the best person who has ever worked for you, and the worst—what made these employees good or bad?

+	−
1.	1.
2.	2.
3.	3.
4.	4.
5.	5.

2. Consider whether the characteristics you've listed are personality traits or work traits.
3. If they are work traits, write them down in the "Brainstorm Work Traits" section of the Job Description Worksheet.
4. If they are personality traits, write down three ways that each trait affects you or your team's work. Now you should be able to translate them into work traits and include them in your worksheet.

PERSONALITY TRAITS	HOW THIS AFFECTS OUR WORK
1.	1. 2. 3.
2.	1. 2. 3.
3.	1. 2. 3.

EXERCISE 2: BRAINSTORM JOB FUNCTIONS

Use this exercise to come up with a list of job functions and begin to figure out which tasks are most important.

1. Give yourself exactly five minutes. In the space below, write down everything that you need the person in this job to do. When your five minutes are up, set aside the list.

Things I NEED this person to do

_____

_____

_____

_____

_____

_____

_____

_____

_____

_____

2. Set your watch for five more minutes. The topic is, "What do I want the person in this job to do?" When your time is up, set aside the second list.

Things I WANT this person to do

_____

_____

_____

_____

_____

_____

_____

_____

_____

_____

3. Take five more minutes to jot down ideas on this topic: "What are other people expecting from the person in this job?"

Things OTHERS need this person to do

_____

_____

_____

_____

_____

_____

_____

_____

4. Now look at your three lists. In the "Job Functions" section of the Job Description Worksheet, write down any tasks that overlap and the number of times they overlap. List all of the remaining items at the end. You now have a fairly complete list of job functions, and the start of a prioritization process!

EXERCISE 3: PRIORITIZE JOB FUNCTIONS

This exercise will help you pare down your list of job functions to the most important priorities.

1. On the Job Description Worksheet, write a letter grade next to each item on your complete list of job functions to indicate the item's relative importance. Items that are most important deserve an "A," while the least important should get a "C."

2. Consulting your graded list, jot a note next to each item about why you graded it as you did. Some of those reasons may include:
   a. Task is the reason the position exists.
   b. Task is best suited to being done by this position.
   c. Task would be nice to have but not critical.
   d. Task would be the _____ (second, third, fourth) thing I would need done right away.
   e. And so on.

3. Now, count your As (the most important rating). At this point, many managers will have either too many or too few "A" level tasks. As a rough guide, you should target ten to 12 tasks to list on your job description. In your mind, all ten or 12 should be absolutely crucial to the job.

4. If you have too many "A" items, repeat step 1 with only the items on your "A" list. Be ruthless, using absolute necessity as the litmus test. If the task is not absolutely necessary, it's a "B" or "C."

5. If you have too few "A" items, look at your "B" list. Which of those items are truly important to the job?

6. Once you've gotten your list down (or up) to ten or 12 items, list those on the Job Description Worksheet, under "Prioritized List of Job Functions."

EXERCISE 4: CREATE COMPELLING BULLET POINTS

Write down one of the functions from your description in the first space on the chart. Use the remaining spaces to consider the results you want from the position, how you would measure success in that function, and how you can make your language more descriptive. Use the answers to each of these questions to make your job function more compelling. Your last pass should result in a strong, interesting bullet point that you can drop right into your job description!

BASIC JOB FUNCTION:	
What are the desired results of this function?	
Revised function that includes these results:	
How would you measure success at this function?	
Revised function that adds measures of success:	
Are you using the strongest, most descriptive language?	
Revised function that uses most descriptive language:	

EXERCISE 5: DRAFT INTERVIEW QUESTIONS

Using a bullet from your job description, this exercise will help you develop an interview question and three follow-up questions that will help you figure out whether applicants can perform that function well.

1. Take a bullet or statement from the job functions section of your job description and determine the results of doing that task well.
2. Formulate an open-ended question to evaluate the candidate's abilities in that area.
3. Based on a few probable answers, create some follow-up questions to probe deeper into the candidate's experience and knowledge.

Job Function: _____

_____
_____
_____

Question _____

_____
_____
_____

Follow-up Question #1 _____

_____
_____
_____

Follow-up Question #2 _____

_____
_____
_____

Follow-up Question #3 _____

_____
_____

JOB DESCRIPTION WORKSHEET

Division/Department:

Location:

Job title:

Reports to: Title:

BIG PICTURE CONSIDERATIONS

1. State of the current economy:

2. Current hiring market:

3. Competition:

SUCCESS AT YOUR COMPANY

1. Mission, vision, and values:

2. Standards measured in performance appraisal tools:

3. Accomplishments noted in reward and recognition programs:

SUCCESS ON YOUR TEAM

Positive Work Traits

1.

2.

3.

4.

5.

Negative Work Traits

1.

2.

3.

4.

5.

JOB FUNCTIONS

•	•	•
•	•	•
•	•	•
•	•	•
•	•	•
•	•	•
•	•	•
•	•	•
•	•	•

Next to each function, write a letter grade indicating importance, "A" being most important and "C" being least important.

PRIORITIZED LIST OF JOB FUNCTIONS

•	•	•
•	•	•
•	•	•
•	•	•

List the ten to 12 most important functions, and designate essential functions with an "E."

QUALIFICATIONS

Education:

Training (licenses, programs, or certificates):

Knowledge Requirements:

Experience:

OTHER REQUIREMENTS

YOUR COMPANY
JOB DESCRIPTION

Job title:

Location:

Division/Department:

Reports to: Title:

JOB SUMMARY

ESSENTIAL FUNCTIONS

-

-

-

-

-

-

-

-

-

-

- Other projects and responsibilities may be added at the company's discretion.

JOB REQUIREMENTS AND QUALIFICATIONS

Education:

Training Requirements (licenses, programs, or certificates):

Knowledge Requirements:

Experience:

OTHER INFORMATION

Special Information (Travel required, physical requirements, on-call schedules, and so on):

-
-
-
-
-

GOLDEN RULES CHECKLIST

STICK TO THE JOB

❏ Are each of the bullets in your description directly relevant to the job?

❏ Does each bullet describe exactly what you need the person to do?

❏ Does the job description focus on desired results rather than how to achieve them?

BE CLEAR

❏ Have you reviewed each bullet for clarity and ease of understanding?

❏ Did you take out any company-specific references or abbreviations?

❏ Have you been careful not to use bigger words or more flowery writing than absolutely necessary?

BE REASONABLE

❏ Have any unreasonable requests slipped into your job description?

❏ Have you stated the desired results of each function or task?

LOOK TO THE FUTURE

❏ Have you reviewed the goals and vision of your company, division, and department?

❏ Have you discussed future plans with your boss or the head of your department?

❏ Are there any changes in policies, laws, or technology that may affect the position for which you are hiring?

❏ Are you up-to-date on publications from organizations, networking groups, or professional societies that may impact how your particular type of work is done?

TELL THE TRUTH

❏ Does the job description accurately reflect the actual work your new employee will do when he or she starts?

❏ Were you careful not to "puff up" your job description in your efforts to make the position sound more compelling or important?

LEGAL ISSUES CHECKLIST

DISCRIMINATION

❏ Are each of the bullets in your description focused solely on the job?

❏ Does your language refer to race, religion, or other protected characteristics?

❏ Is your language gender specific?

❏ Does your language imply any preference regarding age?

❏ Are each of your bullets essential to doing the job (unless otherwise noted)?

❏ Do your bullets describe the desired results of the function rather than how to achieve the results?

AT-WILL EMPLOYMENT

❏ Is there anything in your job description that might lead candidates to believe they will have job security?

❏ Is there anything that would lead applicants to believe that they can be fired only for specific reasons?

❏ Have you promised (or implied) raises or promotions?

IMPLIED CONTRACTS (Making Promises You Cannot Keep)

❏ Did you put anything in the job description that may not actually happen (for any possible reason)?

❏ In your zeal to make the job look attractive, have you crossed the line between truth and false statements?

PRIVACY ISSUES

❏ Does your job description include any reference to candidates' private lives?

❏ Do you mention marital status?

❏ Do you refer to the applicant's political opinions?

❏ Do you make any reference to off-duty conduct?

JOB CLASSIFICATION ISSUES

❏ Does the description lock the company into paying or not paying overtime?

❏ Have you included any references to exempt/nonexempt status without running it by an expert?

Remember: This is an informal checklist and not a substitute for a thorough legal or human resources review.

YOUR COMPANY

JOB POSTING

Job title:

Location:

JOB SUMMARY

ESSENTIAL FUNCTIONS

JOB REQUIREMENTS AND QUALIFICATIONS

ABOUT OUR COMPANY

HOW TO APPLY

YOUR COMPANY
INTERVIEW QUESTION WORKSHEET

Job title:

Location:

Candidate's Name: Date of Interview:

JOB SUMMARY

ESSENTIAL FUNCTIONS

Function Number One:

Question 1:

- Potential Follow-up question:

- Potential Follow-up question:

Function Number Two:

Question 2:

- Potential Follow-up question:

- Potential Follow-up question:

Function Number Three:

Question 3:

- Potential Follow-up question:

- Potential Follow-up question:

Function Number Four:

Question 4:

- Potential Follow-up question:

- Potential Follow-up question:

Function Number Five:

Question 5:

- Potential Follow-up question:

- Potential Follow-up question:

JOB REQUIREMENTS AND QUALIFICATIONS

Does the candidate fulfill your educational requirements (or have equivalent experience)?

Has the candidate fulfilled the training requirements (licenses, programs, or certificates)?

Does the candidate have the specific experience necessary to do the job?

OTHER INFORMATION

Can the candidate meet the other requirements of the job?

- Travel issues

- Work hours

- On-call requirements

- Other

YOUR COMPANY

90-DAY ORIENTATION BLUEPRINT

Employee's Name:	Start Date:
Job Title:	90-Day End Date:

JOB SUMMARY

PRIMARY FUNCTIONS AND DELIVERABLES

Job Function	Short-Term Goal(s)	Resources Available	Time Due

COMMENTS AND EXPECTATIONS AT BEGINNING OF PERIOD

COMMENTS AND RESULTS AT END OF 90 DAYS

Job Function	Short-Term Goal(s)	Results	Comments

Appendix C

Sample Job Descriptions

This appendix includes sample job descriptions for a variety of positions. These are intended as illustrations only: You should not copy these descriptions or cut and paste the language used here. Remember, your job description will be an effective legal and practical tool only if it accurately reflects the position and its essential functions.

POSITION DESCRIPTION
ACCOUNTING SUPERVISOR

JOB SUMMARY

Supervise, plan, and coordinate the activities and operations of the accounting programs; coordinate assigned activities with other departments, divisions, and the general public; and provide highly responsible and complex staff assistance to Managers in the Finance department.

ESSENTIAL FUNCTIONS

- Coordinate the organization, staffing, and operational activities for the assigned accounting programs.

- Participate in the development and implementation of goals, objectives, policies, and priorities for finance activities; identify resource needs; recommend and implement policies and procedures.

- Select, train, motivate, and evaluate personnel; provide or coordinate staff training; work with employees to correct deficiencies; implement discipline and termination procedures.

- Direct, coordinate, and review the work plan for the accounting programs; meet with the staff to identify and resolve problems; assign work activities and projects; monitor work flow; review and evaluate work products, methods, and procedures.

- Oversee accounting procedures including the issuance and completion of purchasing orders, claim vouchers, and travel expenses.

- Review contracts; monitor expenditures and revenues for compliance with contract provisions and appropriate budgets.

- Control and oversee the issuance of warrants; approve claims entered in claim voucher system for processing.

- Review invoices, receipt of deposits, and procedures of recording funds; monitor all financial reports from the general and subsidiary ledgers; assist in reconciliation and summary data reports.

- Establish and maintain a working environment conducive to positive morale, individual style, quality, creativity, and teamwork.

- Supervise data control operations including the approval of documents and batch processing control; implement modifications to improve systems; participate in the development and testing of new systems.

- Coordinate accounting activities with those of other departments; provide staff assistance to other staff; prepare and present staff reports and other necessary correspondence.

JOB REQUIREMENTS AND QUALIFICATIONS

Education and Experience

Graduation from an accredited four-year college or university with a degree in Finance, Accounting, Business, Public Administration, or a related field.

Five or more years of professional related experience in budgeting, accounting, investments, finance, or a related field.

Or any equivalent combination of education, experience, and training that provides the required knowledge and abilities to do the job.

Knowledge Requirements

Knowledge of modern and complex principles and practices of accounting; methods and procedures of claim voucher management including applicable computer applications; computerized financial reporting and management information systems; principles of budget preparation and control; principles of supervision, training, and performance evaluation; pertinent federal, state, and local laws, codes, and regulations.

Ability to plan, organize, direct, and coordinate the work of supervisory and technical personnel; ability to provide leadership, counsel, motivation, and constructive performance reviews to staff, securing their commitment to department and company goals.

Ability to identify and resolve complex problems with vendors, customers, and regulatory agencies; prepare accurate and complete financial statements and reports from accounting data; maintain a variety of financial records and files; understand and interpret the functions of an automated accounting system; select, supervise, train, and evaluate staff; communicate clearly and concisely; understand, interpret, and explain the government procedures and functions of the company; establish and maintain effective working relationships with those contacted in the course of work.

Knowledge of databases and spreadsheet programs utilized; ability to use central financial information system.

Certified Public Accountant preferred.

POSITION DESCRIPTION
BUSINESS MANAGER

JOB SUMMARY

Plan, organize, and implement customer service activities pertaining to facility rental, billing, and other financial service issues; supervise personnel providing customer services; perform related work as required.

ESSENTIAL FUNCTIONS

- Plan, organize, and assign activities of the facility operation function; directly responsible for maintaining positive customer relations and successfully resolving customer complaints and issues.
- Supervise and train facility operation personnel.
- Review and evaluate staff performance; assist in establishing goals and objectives.
- Select and hire new employees.
- Coordinate the preparation, distribution, and receipt of customer bills in a timely fashion.
- Ensure compliance with Company policies and procedures.
- Collect information from the Finance Department regarding delinquent accounts.
- Perform liaison functions between Finance and other departments to ensure efficient service.
- Refer service complaints to appropriate personnel for further investigation.
- Prepare a variety of written reports and materials.
- Assess monetary needs and make recommendations for section budget; assist in development of department operational budget.

JOB REQUIREMENTS AND QUALIFICATIONS

Education

Graduation from an accredited four-year college or university; or a level of education that, together with experience and training, enables the applicant to demonstrate the required knowledge and experience.

Experience

Five or more years of professional related experience.

Knowledge Requirements

Knowledge of customer service techniques.

Knowledge of principles and practices of effective employee supervision.

Knowledge of fundamental accounting principles, procedures, and applications.

Knowledge of facility rental operations and maintenance procedures.

Knowledge of databases and spreadsheet programs utilized by the Company; knowledge of Company's central financial information system; knowledge of applicable information technology relative to service area.

Knowledge of English usage, spelling, grammar, and punctuation.

Ability to maintain cooperative working relationships with a variety of citizens, boards, and Company staff.

Ability to supervise the work of staff including coordinating, assigning, monitoring, and evaluating work; hiring, training, counseling, and disciplining staff; processing grievances.

Ability to analyze and prepare accounting systems, budgets, schedules, reports, policy and procedures manuals, and business correspondence.

Ability to communicate clearly and concisely, orally and in writing.

Ability to exercise sound judgment within established guidelines.

Ability to use word processing and spreadsheet computer applications provided by the Company.

POSITION DESCRIPTION
COMPUTER PROGRAMMER

JOB TITLE: Computer Programmer
DEPARTMENT: IT
REPORTS TO: Director of Computer Services

JOB SUMMARY

Responsible for the application of basic knowledge of programming, logic, and mathematics in the preparation of computer programs.

ESSENTIAL FUNCTIONS

1) Analyze, review, and rewrite programs, using workflow chart and diagram, applying knowledge of computer capabilities, subject matter, and symbolic logic.

2) Convert detailed logical flowchart to language that can be processed by computer.

3) Resolve symbolic formulations, prepare flowcharts and block diagrams, and encode resultant equations for processing.

4) Develop programs from workflowcharts or diagrams, considering computer storage capacity, speed, and intended use of output data.

5) Assist computer operators or system analysts to resolve problems.

6) Assign, coordinate, and review work and activities of programming personnel.

7) Compile and write documentation of program development and revisions.

8) Prepare or receive detailed workflow chart and diagram to illustrate sequence of steps to describe input, output, and logical operation.

9) Revise or direct revision of existing programs to increase operating efficiency or adapt to new requirements.

10) Collaborate with computer manufacturers and other users to develop new programming methods.

11) Train subordinates in programming and program coding.

12) Consult with managerial, engineering, and technical personnel to clarify program intent, identify problems, and suggest changes.

13) Write instructions to guide operating personnel during production runs.

OTHER FUNCTIONS

Program website scripts as needed.

JOB REQUIREMENTS AND QUALIFICATIONS

1. Bachelor's degree in related field or Associate's degree plus two years full-time directly related work experience, or equivalent experience.

2. One additional year of full-time, directly related work experience beyond requirement above, including experience in a 4th generation language.

3. Demonstrated skills in items four and five below may be substituted for education and experience.

4. Thorough knowledge of electronic data processing coding practices necessary for developing programs of instructions for an electronic digital computer and related peripheral equipment.

5. Ability to prepare clear, detailed, and efficient programs of computer instructions using COBOL, CICS Command Level COBOL, or other current industry standard programming languages for optimum machine utilization.

6. Ability to establish and maintain positive working relationships with other employees.

7. Ability to work independently with minimal supervision.

8. Ability to operate mainframe electronic digital computerized systems, including operating systems and applications software.

9. Proficiency in VSE or UNIX/AIX operating systems; PEOPLETOOLS, DELPHI, or POWERBUILDER development tools; COBOL, CICS COBOL, SQR, PEOPLE-CODE, VISUAL BASIC, C/C++, JAVA, or other industry standard Client/Server programming languages; FOCUS, CRYSTAL REPORTS, N/VISION, or similar query/report generator languages recommended.

OTHER INFORMATION

1. Frequently work at fast pace with unscheduled interruptions.

2. Responsibilities occasionally may require an adjusted work schedule, long days, and evening/weekend hours in order to meet deadlines or to access the computer to perform program tests.

3. May move from one work location to another occasionally.

4. This is a public contact position that requires appropriate business apparel.

POSITION DESCRIPTION
DIRECTOR OF HUMAN RESOURCES

JOB SUMMARY

Plan, organize, and direct a variety of complex administrative, technical, and professional work of the human resources functions of the Company. Provide leadership to the Company in designing systems and developing policies for organizational effectiveness and employee satisfaction, including compensation and benefit systems, classification structures, recruitment, employee development and training, performance management, policy administration/compliance, and labor/employee relations.

ESSENTIAL FUNCTIONS

- Serve as a member of senior management on task forces and committees participating in the Company's strategic planning efforts and addressing Company-wide policy and management issues.

- Manage and supervise human resource department to achieve goals within available resources; plan and organize workloads and staff assignments; train, motivate, and evaluate assigned staff; review progress and direct changes as needed.

- Provide leadership and direction in the development of short and long range plans; gather, interpret, and prepare data for studies, reports, and recommendations; coordinate department activities with other departments as needed.

- Provide professional advice to Company officials on human resource and staff development issues.

- Communicate policies and procedures to staff.

- Assure that assigned areas of responsibility are performed within budget; perform cost control activities; monitor revenues and expenditures in assigned area to assure sound fiscal control; prepare annual budget requests; assure effective and efficient use of budgeted funds, personnel, materials, facilities, and time.

- Serve as Company's representative to regional human resources groups.

JOB REQUIREMENTS AND QUALIFICATIONS
Education

Graduation from an accredited four-year college or university with a degree in Human Resources, Business, Communications, or other related field; or a level of education that, together with experience and training, enables the applicant to meet the job requirements.

Experience

Ten or more years of progressively responsible related experience in a position of comparable scope and size to the Company, including hands-on experience in at least two human resources disciplines (Comp, Benefits, Staffing, Labor/Employee Relations, etc.), as well as supervisory experience.

Licenses and Certifications

Professional Human Resources or Senior Professional Human Resources certification preferred. Alternative Dispute Resolution certification and labor union experience desirable.

Knowledge Requirements

Considerable knowledge of current trends and practices of human resources administration; knowledge of employee classification, compensation and benefits, recruitment, selection, training, and labor relations; considerable knowledge of managerial principles, techniques, and practices.

Considerable knowledge of personal computer use, including word processing and spreadsheet programs.

Skill in preparing and administering budgets; skill in planning, directing, and administering human resources programs and systems.

Ability to prepare and analyze comprehensive reports; ability to carry out assigned projects to their completion; ability to communicate effectively verbally and in writing; ability to establish and maintain effective working relationships with employees, company officials, and labor unions; ability to efficiently and effectively administer a human resource system.

Skill in resolving conflicts and gaining cooperation among competing interest groups.

Ability to provide leadership, counsel, motivation, and constructive performance reviews to staff, securing their commitment to the Company's goals.

Ability to articulate and promote the Company's strategic positions, including its core values, to a diverse audience.

Skill in researching complex issues and developing recommended actions.

Ability to plan and organize the work of others; ability to delegate; ability to manage project/activity deadlines of self and others.

POSITION DESCRIPTION
EMPLOYMENT SPECIALIST

JOB PURPOSE

To address agency mission by achieving program objectives in targeted communities. The Employment Specialist works under the supervision of the Area Manager.

ESSENTIAL FUNCTIONS

Design an appropriate plan of service: Deliver meaningful and effective pre-employment services; facilitate job placement according to agency standards; provide effective employment supports, on-site and off; conduct effective follow-up; transport participants to appointments on an as-needed basis.

Communicate with targeted community groups and/or individuals to maximize interest in our mission and services. Communicate with businesses to generate employment opportunities for clients.

Serve as a liaison to our customers.

Compile and maintain documentation to support and justify service intervention.

Efficiently utilize agency resources to effectively respond to program needs, including but not limited to staff time and equipment.

Perform other related duties as required and directed.

JOB QUALIFICATIONS & REQUIREMENTS

Preference to candidate with four-year degree in vocational rehabilitation, human resources, or social services.

Candidate must have insured vehicle and be legally eligible to drive to regular program assignments.

Candidate must be able to respond to diverse physical demands of program assignments.

Candidate must be able to perform the above essential duties in the following manner:

- Work independently, using independent judgment.
- Maintain knowledge of vocational rehabilitation and local businesses.
- Be professional in dress, speech, and mannerisms.
- Communicate effectively in program mediums.
- Respond to customer needs.
- Work with a flexible schedule and demonstrate effective time management.

JOB DESCRIPTION
EVENTS COORDINATOR

JOB SUMMARY

This position provides assistance in managing the events facility in a cost-effective and efficient manner. The events coordinator assists with planning, organizing, implementing, promoting, and evaluating comprehensive year-round events and services that meet public demand. The coordinator must possess excellent interpersonal skills and tact, organizational and planning skills, and the ability to respond to customers that may be upset or under stress. Duties are often performed under stressful situations with rigid deadlines. This work requires a great deal of interpersonal activity with a sales and marketing orientation.

ESSENTIAL FUNCTIONS

- Develop and direct reservations and bookings for special events.
- Perform assigned administrative tasks for special events such as contact with clients, availability of dates, correspondence, and tours of facility.
- Respond to public inquiries and provide other supportive services necessary to operation of center.
- Greet customers and provide assistance as needed; answer telephone calls and make contacts with potential customers.
- Assure completion of all documents related to an event and assure that payment is made; assure effective coordination during an event.
- Prepare and mail flyers and brochures.

OTHER JOB DUTIES

Act as Events Supervisor, as needed.

JOB REQUIREMENTS AND QUALIFICATIONS
Education and Training

College course work in hotel/motel management or related field and two years full-time hospitality work experience; or any combination of education and experience which would provide the applicant with the desired skills, knowledge, and ability required to perform the job.

Knowledge Requirements

- Knowledge of special events planning and coordination.
- Ability to perform tasks such as facility scheduling, public information, and administrative skills.
- Ability to communicate effectively, both orally and in writing.
- Ability to organize and coordinate part-time and support personnel.
- Ability to establish and maintain effective working relationships with other employees, vendors, and the public.

OTHER INFORMATION

The coordinator is required to work weekends and other irregular hours as deemed necessary.

The statements contained herein reflect general details as necessary to describe the principal functions of this job, the level of knowledge and skill typically required, and the scope of responsibility, but should not be considered an all-inclusive listing of work requirements.

POSITION DESCRIPTION
EXECUTIVE SECRETARY

JOB SUMMARY

To perform a variety of responsible, confidential, and complex administrative, technical, and secretarial duties. Act as a liaison with other departments, staff, outside agencies, and the general public. Ensure the efficient operation of the office.

ESSENTIAL FUNCTIONS

1. Act as confidential administrative assistant in the executive department, managing calendars and schedules, screening callers, and arranging appointments, meetings, and conferences, as directed.

2. Assist in the preparation of budgets, prepare expenditure estimates, and gather and organize supporting data. Monitor individual accounts within these budgets to track expenditures and alert to potential overspending.

3. Design, establish, and maintain a management information system, including physical and electronic files, for the department. Prepare reports as directed.

4. Act as office manager and coordinator. As directed, supervise, train, and evaluate other secretarial or clerical staff within the department.

5. Respond to inquiries on the telephone and in person with visitors to the executive department. Provide information and assistance to the public in a courteous manner and with sensitivity to the diversity of a multicultural clientele. Resolve complaints within scope of information and authority and refer to others, as appropriate.

6. Transcribe dictated or written materials. Take minutes at meetings, as required.

7. Initiate correspondence on a variety of matters requiring an in-depth understanding of department policies, procedures, and company ordinances. Format, create, produce, and edit correspondence and other written materials.

8. Operate office equipment including copiers, facsimile machines, and computers; input and retrieve data and text; and organize and maintain disk storage and filing.

JOB QUALIFICATIONS AND REQUIREMENTS

1. Must have or be able to quickly acquire knowledge of departmental program structure (mission, goals, and objectives), department polices, and procedures.

2. Must have Associate's degree, or comparable experience, as evidence of a broad education and an ability to deal with diverse situations and people.

3. Must have a minimum of six years office management or increasingly responsible secretarial/administrative experience, preferably as a confidential secretary. Previous experience in local area is a plus.

4. Some supervisory experience is desirable.

5. Must type a minimum of 60 words per minute with accuracy in a setting with many interruptions. Must transcribe from dictation equipment, handwritten drafts, or verbal dictation. Shorthand skills are desirable.

6. Must be able to operate a memory typewriter and a personal computer and learn quickly to use the software programs of the department.

7. Must have a sound knowledge and ability in business correspondence and an ability to proofread for grammar, spelling, and punctuation with a high degree of accuracy.

8. Must be able to do basic accounting and mathematical computations with a high degree of accuracy (for example, to calculate travel expenses or assist with budget calculations).

9. Must possess a valid Washington State driver's license.

10. Pubic Notary designation is desirable.

11. Must be able to handle multiple interruptions and adjustments to priorities throughout the day.

12. Must be able to communicate effectively with diverse, and sometimes irate, individuals and to handle calmly and efficiently situations ranging from routine to emergency.

13. Excellent memory and organizational ability, in order to set priorities, organize workload, handle multiple responsibilities, and meet deadlines.

USE OF TOOLS
Standard office equipment including personal computer, memory typewriter, multiline telephone system, fax machine, copier, 10-key calculator, and dictation equipment.

OTHER
The statements contained in this job description reflect general details as necessary to describe the principal functions of this job, the level of knowledge and skill typically required, and the scope of responsibility. It should not be considered an all-inclusive listing of work requirements. Individuals may perform other duties as assigned, including work in other functional areas to cover absences or relief, to equalize peak work periods, or otherwise to balance the workload.

XYZ FLIGHT SCHOOL
POSITION: FLIGHT INSTRUCTOR

JOB SUMMARY

Provide flight, simulator, and ground instruction in accordance with XYZ Flight School and FAA regulations and procedures. Prepare schedules, maintain records, and ensure that course standards, training requirements, and objectives are met by each student in each flight course.

ESSENTIAL FUNCTIONS

Perform flight instructor duties authorized by the Federal Aviation Regulations in accordance with the approved Training Course Outline.

Ensure all students understand and practice all aspects of XYZ Flight School's Aviation Safety Program.

Regularly schedule each assigned student to ensure satisfactory progress through the course and immediately inform supervisor of any delays in training or satisfactory progress.

Responsible for accurately maintaining all appropriate records to include student training record, student logbook, and computer records.

Ensure that course standards, training requirements, and objectives are met by all assigned students as stipulated in the applicable Training Course Outline.

Initiate stage check and requests for assigned students.

Responsible for the timely course completion of all flight students assigned, including completion of required paperwork and assignment of final course grade.

Monitor the maintenance condition of the training aircraft and inform XYZ Flight School maintenance personnel of any questionable items.

Recommend curriculum and courseware improvements when appropriate and develop new curriculum or courseware as assigned.

File incident reports as necessary to report any observed safety violations or situations that may affect the safety of flight.

Attend administrative, standardization, in-service training, and instructor development meetings as assigned.

Other duties as assigned.

JOB REQUIREMENTS AND QUALIFICATIONS

1. Licenses and Certifications

FAA Certified Flight Instructor, Airplane Single Engine Land, Instrument Airplane.

Must hold a current FAA Class I or Class II Medical Certificate.

2. Knowledge Requirements

Aircraft piloting skills, including familiarity with and ability to perform required flight maneuvers and procedures.

Knowledge of and ability to apply effective instructional technique in the classroom and in flight.

Knowledge of appropriate Federal Aviation Regulations

Ability to work well under pressure in fast-paced and noisy environment while exercising sound judgment at all times.

3. Productivity/Performance Standards

Must perform an average of 46 instructional hours per two-week pay period.

Must maintain 80% pass rate for final review and stage checks.

4. Equipment Requirements

Must provide personal equipment for instruction as appropriate to include headsets, instrument covers, current navigational charts, Practical Test Standards, and other technical publications.

XYZ Flight School will provide Flight School–specific program materials including student workbooks, aircraft manuals, Flight Operations Manual, Standardization Manuals, and checklists.

Must comply with Flight Training Uniform dress code.

POSITION DESCRIPTION
MANAGER, COMPETITIVE INTELLIGENCE

JOB SUMMARY

The Competitive Intelligence (CI) Manager will coordinate the activities of the CI team and be responsible for its output. This will involve working closely with senior management to identify the CI needs of the company; developing and leading a team of skilled professional analysts; being responsible for the quality of CI output; presenting intelligence generated by the department to senior management; managing the efforts of the CI team in conjunction with other intelligence and data-gathering units of the company to limit overlap and optimize the information-gathering and analytical capacity of the company as a whole.

ESSENTIAL FUNCTIONS

- Oversee and be responsible for the CI function of XYZ Corporation. Working with the senior management, product development, and marketing teams, set objectives for intelligence gathering and create a feasible schedule for the collection and analysis of data.

- Lead the CI group. Supervise the collection and analysis activities of the group's analysts, assigning projects and authorizing specific data-gathering exercises. Working with corporate counsel, develop a compliance plan for the Economic Espionage Act of 1996 and ensure that all XYZ's intelligence and information-gathering activities are undertaken using ethical and legal techniques.

- Assess the resource requirements of the CI group. Ensure it has the resources necessary to gather and analyze data. Procure equipment, hire and train staff, and retain consultants as required, within the group's budget.

- Communicate with other departments to ensure an effective flow of information to and from the CI group. While the CI group is primarily responsible for analyzing competitive information, data should come from the entire company; effective two-way communication is the responsibility of the CI manager. Ensure all staff at XYZ Corporation is aware of the CI group and able to pass along information quickly and easily. While the CI group's output is primarily designed to aid decision making by senior managers, the CI group will also provide actionable intelligence to other units when required.

- Supervise the CI group staff. Ensure that the staff acquire and maintain appropriate skills and are able to develop professionally.
- Manage the CI group budget.
- Take responsibility for the CI group's outgoing analysis and conclusions. Make regular presentations of findings to senior management and other client groups.

JOB REQUIREMENTS AND QUALIFICATIONS

- Bachelor's degree (MBA preferred).
- At least eight years of experience in competitive analysis in the XYZ industry. Experience with marketing is also important.
- Proven leadership skills: experience as a project leader or supervisor of professional staff.
- Excellent written and oral communication skills; experience working with senior managers and making boardroom presentations.

POSITION DESCRIPTION
NETWORK ANALYST

JOB SUMMARY

Under general supervision, the network analyst designs, installs, implements, administers, supports, documents, and maintains network computer systems, PC Servers, and the Company's IBM AS/400 computers.

ESSENTIAL FUNCTIONS

Develop and recommend policies for IBM AS/400, PC Servers, networking infrastructure, system security, and services.

Plan and implement complex and routine short- and long-range projects related to network systems, software, hardware, upgrades, and infrastructure.

Monitor system performance for connectivity, job completion, backups, night jobs, restoring files, etc.

Monitor system, using system tools to predict system performance. Develop and make recommendations about replacing hardware or software to meet demands and increase performance.

Prepare and present project and network- and system-related budgets.

Ensure that users always have access to network systems, applications, and services. Schedule any network maintenance and server downtime to be performed during off-peak hours. Properly notify users of any scheduled outages.

Carry out routine and emergency technical installation and maintenance of IBM AS/400s, network hardware and software, servers, operating systems, storage devices, switches, routers, and end-user equipment.

Create and maintain a shared Change Management System to track changes to hardware and software on the AS/400, PC Servers, and network hardware and software. Communicate network, server, and system changes, new features, documentation, manuals, instructions, maps, and charts. Schedule and install Program Temporary Fixes (PTF) and Microsoft application Service Packs.

Install and maintain IBM AS/400, network operating systems, and network-based applications. Provide support, information, consultation, and training to departments, sections, and individual users.

Determine and monitor technical status of network and plan for future modifications, connections, and equipment purchases.

Establish, maintain, and review IBM AS/400 and network data protection, anti-virus, and security policies, backup procedures, and methods.

Ensure that Company network systems connect with and work reliably and compatibly with internal and external network systems, databases, and Internet service providers.

Provide user-level network services such as designing security policy, setting up groups, assigning passwords and accounts, administering data sharing, and transmission protocols. Provide ongoing support to the Computer Systems Technicians, completing work orders and setting up and installing hardware, software, printers, and peripherals.

Troubleshoot problems noted in the operation of the AS/400 hardware, software, and operating system. Initiate the necessary revisions in the system for problem resolution. Provide responsive and effective service and problem resolution to network users.

Work closely with ISD staff to perform backups; create test environments and application updates; and apply PFT's to Company applications.

JOB REQUIREMENTS AND QUALIFICATIONS
Education and Experience

Bachelor's degree in computer science, MIS, or a related field and a minimum of two years of increasingly responsible experience in the design, analysis, implementation, and support of complex network systems. Network administration and data communication coordination experience preferred. Certification in network technology currently used by the Company highly desirable. In place of the above, candidates may demonstrate possession of equivalent and relevant combinations of experience, education, and training that demonstrates possession of the knowledge, skills, and abilities listed above and establishes ability to perform the duties listed.

Knowledge and Training Requirements

The network analyst must understand:

- Ethernet and Token ring networks
- Network protocols such as TCP/IP, SNA, and interoperability standards
- WAN transport protocols such as Frame relay, SDLC, ISDN, T1, and ATM
- Intranet and Internet concepts, protocols, and connection options
- Network security models and methods

- Microsoft networking components such as win2000, NT 4.0, DHCP, WINS, SMS, IIS, SQL server, Exchange, and client server applications
- Software licensing standards documentation and tracking systems
- Network backup methods and emergency/disaster recovery for Windows NT servers and IBM AS/400
- PC virus protection, detection, removal, and prevention
- Networking, routers, switches, hubs, WAP, and wireless bridges by IBM, Cisco, and others
- IBM AS/400 Control Language (CL).

OTHER INFORMATION

A valid Driver's License is required.

A criminal history and background check is required and must be successfully completed prior to employment.

Work such as major installations or software upgrades must frequently be done during evenings, weekends, or holidays to minimize disruptions. A network analyst may be called in to work with short notice in emergency conditions.

JOB DESCRIPTION
PROCUREMENT SPECIALIST

JOB SUMMARY

Perform routine and complex clerical work in coordinating the Company's formal bid process and all "Requests for Proposals" (RFPs); manage project retainage payment process. Assist with general purchasing activities related to Company purchase orders.

ESSENTIAL FUNCTIONS

- Coordinate formal bids and RFPs by reviewing specifications, scheduling opening dates, arranging advertising, and maintaining files.
- Maintain and edit standard forms used in bid/RFP specifications.
- Deposit money received from the sale of bid specifications.
- Administer retainage contract files; maintain documents and authorize release of retainage upon receipt of all required documentation from the administering department.
- Prepare purchase orders and requisitions for division.
- Maintain vendor file for purchase order system by checking addresses on invoices and performing some follow-up with vendors.
- Maintain procurement records such as items or services purchased, costs, delivery, product quality or performance, and inventories; compile data for internal reports.
- Approve invoices for payment; prepare checks.
- Maintain a variety of material, supply, equipment, and other lists of items required by the Company; maintain lists of vendors supplying said items.
- Check all invoices to ensure correct price; follow through to insure that materials ordered have been received; examine condition of materials received.
- Interview vendors in person or by telephone to obtain information relative to product, price, and ability of vendor to produce product, service, and delivery date.
- Keep records pertaining to items purchased, costs, and delivery; prepare monthly reports.

JOB REQUIRMENTS AND QUALIFICATIONS
Education and Experience

- Graduation from high school or GED equivalent.
- Four or more years of responsible related experience in general clerical skills with some bookkeeping and accounting skills.
- Or any equivalent combination of education, experience, and training that provides the required knowledge, skills, and abilities.

Knowledge Requirements

- Considerable knowledge of purchasing methods and procedures.
- Working knowledge of sources of supplies, price trends, and grades or quality of materials and equipment.
- Working knowledge of the laws and ordinances governing the purchase of goods and services.
- Working knowledge of personal computers including word processing, database, and spreadsheet applications.

The successful applicant will also have the ability to:

- analyze and process purchasing requisitions and vouchers and make purchasing decisions accordingly
- maintain complex purchasing and inventory records
- establish and maintain effective working relationships with employees, other departments, vendors, and the public
- communicate effectively, orally and in writing.
- listen and ascertain the needs of customers
- find and communicate accurate information concerning process, policies, and procedures to customers
- respond to customers tactfully and courteously.

JOB DESCRIPTION
RECEPTIONIST

JOB SUMMARY

The Receptionist handles customer inquiries both in person and on the phone, and provides information and assistance to staff and the public according to established procedures. This position is also responsible for computer support, photocopying, filing, mailing, and other clerical duties to support the other staff members in a busy office environment.

ESSENTIAL FUNCTIONS

- Answer 3-line telephone to assist the public with program and course information, registration, and directions to facilities and events.

- Perform in-person reception duties for events and activities that take place at the company.

- Register customers in courses; receive cash, check, and charge payments; put money in cash register. May be responsible for balancing the till.

- Compose, type, proofread, and copy memos and other documents. May assist in publishing company documents as needed.

- Maintain basic logs and perform data entry.

- Maintain files on a variety of subjects; mail distribution, news releases, and other administrative duties as assigned.

- Become cross-trained on other administrative duties.

JOB REQUIREMENTS AND QUALIFICATIONS

- Ability to maintain good working relationship with customers, employees, and department staff.

- Ability to accurately type 50 words per minute.

- Knowledge of and experience with IBM-compatible computers, word processing software, and other office equipment. Working knowledge of Word for Windows 6.0 and/or PageMaker is a plus.

- Effective oral and written communication skills, including the ability to clearly express thoughts to others and exchange information.

- Clear speaking voice in the English language.

- Ability to maintain confidentiality of files and other documents.

- Ability to work with money and cash receipts; must be bondable.
- Ability to dress in a professional manner.
- Valid driver's license and good driving record.
- Demonstrated record of good work attendance and reliability.
- Flexible in work habits and work schedule.
- This position requires a professional demeanor and an orientation towards customer service.

POSITION DESCRIPTION
REGIONAL SALES DIRECTOR

JOB SUMMARY

Manage sales of the company's products and services in a fairly large geographic area. Establish effective communications with appropriate executives and managers to ensure proper sensitivity to sales needs. Position typically has five Sales Managers or Telesales/Internet Sales Managers as direct reports. Usually requires nine to 12 years of product sales experience with two or more years of field sales management experience. The incumbent is likely to report to the Chief Field Sales Executive or Chief Field Operations Executive.

ESSSENTIAL FUNCTIONS

Manage an assigned geographic sales area or product line to maximize sales revenues and meet corporate objectives:

- Accurately forecast annual, quarterly, and monthly revenue streams.
- Develop specific plans to ensure revenue growth in all company's products.
- Provide quarterly assessments of sales staff's productivity.
- Direct professional account management activities.
- Coordinate proper company resources to ensure efficient and stable software sales.

Manage and develop sales and sales support staff:

- Manage personnel activities of staff (i.e. hire, train, coach, appraise, reward, motivate, discipline, recommend termination as necessary, etc.).
- Educate sales unit in terms of sales tactics.
- Evaluate effectiveness of district managers; recommend necessary changes.

Establish and manage effective programs and seminars to address the following issues:

- New account sales and growth to base through sales force.
- Sales of emerging products and multiproduct sales.
- Improved seminar presentations.
- Proactive competitive strategies and targeted sales campaigns.
- Proper use and level of sales support.
- Management of expenses of the area at a reasonable level.
- Business/financial issues on contracts.

Perform sales activities on major accounts and negotiate sales price and discounts through the head of sales.

JOB REQUIREMENTS AND QUALIFICATIONS

Education and Work Experience

Bachelor's degree in business, sales, or marketing; or equivalent training in business or sales management. Typically requires seven or more years of experience in product sales with at least two years of experience in sales management.

Specialized Knowledge, Equipment, and Applications

Excellent knowledge of company's products, software pricing practices, and selling skills. Effective management skills with ability to manage a major portion of the company's field sales operations. Excellent time management, communications, decision-making, human relations, presentation, and organization skills. Professional appearance and presentation required. Familiarity with PCs and various software applications. Heavy telephone usage required.

OTHER INFORMATION

Extensive travel required.

POSITION DESCRIPTION
SENIOR DIRECTOR, STAFFING

JOB SUMMARY

The Senior Director of Staffing is responsible for developing the staffing function to fulfill Company XYZ's short- and long-term business plans. The Senior Director will provide focus, direction, and consistency of core recruitment practices while coordinating and participating in large practice-based recruitment initiatives. This individual will also be responsible, in conjunction with human resources liaisons and regional and divisional directors of human resources, for the management of internal and external resources dedicated to staffing/recruitment.

ESSENTIAL FUNCTIONS

In partnership with the human resources liaisons and regional and divisional directors of human resources, conduct staffing needs assessments and develop staffing plans for each practice, region, and division.

MANAGE A TEAM OF STAFFING PROFESSIONALS

Implement the staffing plan, developing high-quality staffing processes and tools in order to:

- Build Company XYZ's brand as a place to work.
- Create and implement selection strategies that lead to sustainable, high-performing teams.
- Build upon Company XYZ's diversity and inclusion programs to assure that the candidate selection pool is populated with people of many and varied viewpoints.
- Develop robust sourcing strategy that ensures strong candidate flow for Company XYZ's current and future vacancies ,and rationalizes costs incurred in the creative use of external search providers.
- Monitor performance, provide direction, and take corrective action when needed for all preferred external staffing vendors.
- Manage staffing vendor contact negotiations.
- Recruit executive-level candidates.
- Create and implement College Recruiting Program.

Develop, enhance, and drive key HR programs, processes, and practices on a global basis, aligning HR with the Company's overall business objectives and building accountability within the organization.

JOB QUALIFICATIONS AND REQUIREMENTS
Education

Bachelor's degree or equivalent in Human Resources or related field is required. An advanced degree in Human Resources or Business Administration is highly desirable.

EXPERIENCE

Ten to 12 (or more) years of progressive HR generalist responsibility in leading-edge, high technology companies, including a minimum of 3-5 years in a senior HR management and business partner role with global staffing responsibility. Experience within the software industry, ideally within the enterprise software arena, is a strong plus.

The ideal candidate will possess the following:

- A combination of large and small company experience
- Strong business acumen and the ability to understand the business needs of Company XYZ.
- Demonstrated ability to work effectively with, present to, and influence Senior Management and Executive Staff levels.
- Strong consulting, negotiation, problem resolution, mediation, and interpersonal skills.
- Proven ability to work within a fast-paced, high-change environment.
- Demonstrate sound business judgment and the ability to work successfully with all levels of professionals, backgrounds, and perspectives.
- Exceptional leadership and management skills and the ability to motivate, develop, and inspire a team while creating a highly empowered organization.
- A compelling leadership style that includes exceptional people management skills, program management, business and technology expertise, and the ability to inspire confidence in Company XYZ and its products.
- Ability to quickly build credibility and rapport with the HR and Company XYZ leadership.

Appendix D

Laws and Agencies

State Laws Prohibiting Discrimination in Employment

State	Law applies to employers with	Private employers may not make employment decisions based on			
		Age (protected ages, if specified)	Ancestry or national origin	Disability	AIDS/HIV
Alabama Ala. Code §§ 21-7-1, 25-1-20	20 or more employees	✓ (40 and older)			
Alaska Alaska Stat. §§ 18.80.220, 47.30.865	One or more employees	✓ (40 and older)	✓	Physical and mental	✓
Arizona Ariz. Rev. Stat. § 41-1461	15 or more employees	✓ (40 and older)	✓	Physical	✓
Arkansas Ark. Code Ann. §§ 16-12-101, 11-4-601, 11-5-403	9 or more employees		✓	Physical and mental	
California Cal. Gov't. Code §§ 12920, 12941; Cal. Lab. Code § 1101	5 or more employees	✓ (40 and older)	✓	Physical and mental	✓
Colorado Colo. Rev. Stat. §§ 24-34-301, 24-34-401, 27-10-115	One or more employees	✓ (40 to 70)	✓	Physical, mental, and learning	✓
Connecticut Conn. Gen. Stat. Ann. §§ 46a-51, 46a-60	3 or more employees	✓ (40 and older)	✓	Present or past physical, mental, or learning	✓
Delaware Del. Code Ann. tit. 19, § 710	4 or more employees	✓ (40 to 70)	✓	Physical or mental	✓
District of Columbia D.C. Code Ann. §§ 2-1401.01, 7-1703.03	One or more employees	✓ (18 and older)	✓	Physical or mental	✓
Florida Fla. Stat. Ann. §§ 760.01, 760.50, 448.075	15 or more employees	✓	✓	"Handicap"	✓

State Laws Prohibiting Discrimination in Employment, con't

Private employers may not make employment decisions based on

Gender	Marital status	Pregnancy, childbirth, and related medical conditions	Race or color	Religion or creed	Sexual orientation	Genetic testing information	Additional protected categories
✓	✓ (Includes changes in status)	✓ Parenthood	✓	✓			• Mental illness
✓			✓	✓		✓	
✓		✓	✓	✓		✓¹	
✓	✓	✓	✓	✓	✓	✓	• Gender identity • Medical condition • Political activities or affiliations
✓		✓	✓	✓			• Lawful conduct outside of work • Mental illness
✓	✓	✓	✓	✓	✓	✓	• Mental retardation
✓	✓	✓	✓	✓		✓	
✓	✓	✓ Parenthood	✓	✓	✓		• Enrollment in vocational, professional, or college education • Family duties • Perceived race • Personal appearance • Political affiliation • Smoker
✓	✓		✓	✓			• Family status • Sickle cell trait • Breastfeeding at work

¹Employees covered by FLSA

State Laws Prohibiting Discrimination in Employment, con't

State	Law applies to employers with	Private employers may not make employment decisions based on			
		Age (protected ages, if specified)	Ancestry or national origin	Disability	AIDS/HIV
Georgia Ga. Code Ann. §§ 34-6A-1, 34-1-23, 34-5-1	15 or more employees (disability) 10 or more employees (gender)	✓ (40 to 70)		Physical or mental	
Hawaii Haw. Rev. Stat. § 378-1	One or more employees	✓	✓	Physical or mental	✓
Idaho Idaho Code § 67-5909	5 or more employees	✓ (40 and older)	✓	Physical or mental	
Illinois 775 Ill. Comp. Stat. §§ 5/1-101, 5/2-101; Ill. Admin. Code tit. 56, § 5210.110	15 or more employees	✓ (40 and older)	✓	Physical or mental	✓
Indiana Ind. Code Ann. §§ 22-9-1-1, 22-9-2-1	6 or more employees	✓ (40 to 70)	✓	Physical or mental (15 or more employees)	
Iowa Iowa Code § 216.1	4 or more employees	✓ (18 or older)	✓	Physical or mental	✓
Kansas Kan. Stat. Ann. §§ 44-1001, 44-1111, 44-1125, 65-6002(e)	4 or more employees	✓ (18 or older)	✓	Physical or mental	✓
Kentucky Ky. Rev. Stat. Ann. §§ 344.040, 207.130, 342.197	8 or more employees	✓ (40 or older)	✓	Physical	✓
Louisiana La. Rev. Stat. Ann. §§ 23:301 to 23:352	20 or more employees	✓ (40 or older)	✓	Physical or mental	

State Laws Prohibiting Discrimination in Employment, con't

Private employers may not make employment decisions based on

Gender	Marital status	Pregnancy, childbirth, and related medical conditions	Race or color	Religion or creed	Sexual orientation	Genetic testing information	Additional protected categories
✓[2]							
✓	✓	✓ Breastfeeding	✓	✓	✓	✓	• Arrest and court record (unless there is a conviction directly related to job)
✓		✓	✓	✓			
✓	✓	✓	✓	✓			• Arrest record • Expunged juvenile record • Citizen status • Military status • Unfavorable military discharge • Victim of domestic violence or sexual assault
✓			✓	✓			
✓		✓	✓	✓		✓	
✓			✓	✓		✓	• Military status
✓			✓	✓			• Smoker or nonsmoker
✓		✓ (Applies to employers with 25 or more employees)	✓	✓		✓	• Sickle cell trait

[2] Wage discrimination only

State Laws Prohibiting Discrimination in Employment, con't

State	Law applies to employers with	Age (protected ages, if specified)	Ancestry or national origin	Disability	AIDS/HIV
	Private employers may not make employment decisions based on				
Maine Me. Rev. Stat. Ann. tit. 5, §§ 4551, 4571	One or more employees	✓	✓	Physical or mental	
Maryland Md. Code 1957 Art. 49B, § 15	15 or more employees	✓	✓	Physical or mental	
Massachusetts Mass. Gen. Laws ch. 151B, § 1	6 or more employees	✓ (40 or older)	✓	Physical or mental	✓
Michigan Mich. Comp. Laws §§ 37.1201, 37.2201, 37.1103	One or more employees	✓	✓	Physical or mental	✓
Minnesota Minn. Stat. Ann. §§ 363A.03, 363A.08, 181.974	One or more employees	✓ (18 or older)	✓	Physical or mental	✓
Mississippi Miss. Code Ann. § 33-1-15					
Missouri Mo. Rev. Stat. §§ 213.010, 191.665, 375.1306	6 or more employees	✓ (40 to 70)	✓	Physical or mental	✓
Montana Mont. Code Ann. §§ 49-2-101, 49-2-303	One or more employees	✓	✓	Physical or mental	
Nebraska Neb. Rev. Stat. §§ 48-1101, 48-1001, 20-168	15 or more employees	✓ (40 to 70) (Applies to employers with 25 or more employees)	✓	Physical or mental	✓
Nevada Nev. Rev. Stat. Ann. §§ 613.310 and following	15 or more employees	✓ (40 or older)	✓	Physical or mental	
New Hampshire N.H. Rev. Stat. Ann. §§ 354-A2 and following, 141-H:3	6 or more employees	✓	✓	Physical or mental	
New Jersey N.J. Stat. Ann. §§ 10:5-1 to 10:5-12; 34:6B-1	One or more employees	✓ (18 to 70)	✓	Past or present physical or mental	✓

State Laws Prohibiting Discrimination in Employment, con't

Private employers may not make employment decisions based on

Gender	Marital status	Pregnancy, childbirth, and related medical conditions	Race or color	Religion or creed	Sexual orientation	Genetic testing information	Additional protected categories
✓		✓	✓	✓	✓	✓	• Past workers' compensation claim • Past whistleblowing
✓	✓	✓	✓	✓	✓	✓	
✓	✓		✓	✓	✓	✓	• Military service • Arrests
✓	✓	✓	✓	✓		✓	• Height or weight • Arrest record
✓	✓	✓	✓	✓	✓	✓	• Gender identity • Member of local commission • Perceived sexual orientation • Receiving public assistance • Military status (all employers) • No other protected categories unless employer receives public funding
✓		✓	✓	✓		✓	
✓	✓	✓	✓	✓			
✓	✓	✓	✓	✓		✓	
✓		✓	✓	✓	✓	✓	• Lawful use of any product when not at work • Use of service animal
✓	✓	✓	✓	✓	✓	✓	
✓	✓ (Includes domestic partner)	✓	✓	✓	✓	✓	• Hereditary cellular or blood trait • Military service or status • Smoker or nonsmoker

State Laws Prohibiting Discrimination in Employment, con't

State	Law applies to employers with	Age (protected ages, if specified)	Ancestry or national origin	Disability	AIDS/HIV
		Private employers may not make employment decisions based on			
New Mexico N.M. Stat. Ann. § 28-1-7	4 or more employees	✓ (40 or older) (applies to employers with 20 or more employees)	✓	Physical or mental	
New York N.Y. Exec. Law § 296; N.Y. Lab. Law § 201-d	4 or more employees	✓ (18 and over)	✓	Physical or mental	✓
North Carolina N.C. Gen. Stat. §§ 143-422.2, 168A-1, 95-28.1, 130A-148	15 or more employees	✓	✓	Physical or mental	✓
North Dakota N.D. Cent. Code §§ 14-02.4-01, 34-01-17	One or more employees	✓ (40 or older)	✓	Physical or mental	
Ohio Ohio Rev. Code Ann. §§ 4111.17, 4112.01	4 or more employees	✓ (40 or older)	✓	Physical, mental, or learning	
Oklahoma Okla. Stat. Ann. tit. 25, § 1301; tit. 36, § 3614.2; tit. 40, § 500; tit. 44, § 208	15 or more employees	✓ (40 or older)	✓	Physical or mental	
Oregon Or. Rev. Stat. §§ 659A.100 and following, 659A.303	One or more employees	✓ (18 or older)	✓	Physical or mental (Applies to employers with 6 or more employees)	
Pennsylvania 43 Pa. Cons. Stat. Ann. § 953	4 or more employees	✓ (40 to 70)	✓	Physical or mental	
Rhode Island R.I. Gen. Laws §§ 28-6-17, 28-5-11, 2-28-10, 23-6-22, 23-20.7.1-1	4 or more employees	✓ (40 or older)	✓	Physical or mental	✓
South Carolina S.C. Code Ann. §§ 1-13-20 and following	15 or more employees	✓ (40 or older)	✓	Physical or mental	

State Laws Prohibiting Discrimination in Employment, con't

Private employers may not make employment decisions based on

Gender	Marital status	Pregnancy, childbirth, and related medical conditions	Race or color	Religion or creed	Sexual orientation	Genetic testing information	Additional protected categories
✓	✓ (Applies to employers with 50 or more employees)	✓	✓	✓	✓³		• Gender identity (employers with 15 or more employees) • Serious medical condition
✓	✓	✓	✓	✓	✓	✓	• Lawful use of any product when not at work • Military status • Observance of Sabbath • Political activities
✓			✓	✓		✓	• Lawful use of any product when not at work • Military service • Sickle cell trait
✓	✓	✓	✓	✓			• Lawful conduct outside of work • Receiving public assistance
✓		✓	✓	✓			
✓			✓	✓		✓	• Military service • Smoker or nonsmoker
✓	✓	✓	✓	✓		✓	
✓		✓	✓	✓			• Familial status • GED rather than high school diploma
✓		✓	✓	✓	✓	✓	• Domestic abuse victim • Gender identity or expression
✓		✓	✓	✓			

³ Employers with 15 or more employees

State Laws Prohibiting Discrimination in Employment, con't

State	Law applies to employers with	Age (protected ages, if specified)	Ancestry or national origin	Disability	AIDS/HIV
	Private employers may not make employment decisions based on				
South Dakota S.D. Codified Laws Ann. §§ 20-13-10, 60-12-15, 60-2-20, 62-1-17	One or more employees		✓	Physical, mental, and learning	
Tennessee Tenn. Code Ann. §§ 4-21-102, 4-21-401 and following, 8-50-103, 50-2-202	8 or more employees	✓ (40 or older)	✓	Physical or mental	
Texas Tex. Lab. Code Ann. §§ 21.002, 21.101, 21.401	15 or more employees	✓ (40 or older)	✓	Physical or mental	
Utah Utah Code Ann. § 34A-5-106	15 or more employees	✓ (40 or older)	✓	Follows federal law	✓
Vermont Vt. Stat. Ann. tit. 21, § 495; tit. 18, § 9333	One or more employees	✓ (18 or older)	✓	Physical, mental, or learning	✓
Virginia Va. Code Ann. §§ 2.2-3900, 40.1-28.6, 51.5-3	Law applies to all employers	✓	✓	Physical or mental	
Washington Wash. Rev. Code Ann. §§ 49.60.040, 49.60.172 and following, 49.12.175, 49.44.090; Wash. Admin. Code 162-30-020	8 or more employees	✓ (40 or older)	✓	Physical, mental, or sensory; use of a service animal	✓
West Virginia W.Va. Code §§ 5-11-3, 5-11-9, 21-5B-1	12 or more employees	✓ (40 or older)	✓	Physical or mental	✓
Wisconsin Wis. Stat. Ann. §§ 111.32 and following	One or more employees	✓ (40 or older)	✓	Physical or mental	✓
Wyoming Wyo. Stat. §§ 27-9-105, 19-11-104	2 or more employees	✓ (40 or older)	✓		

‹ Equal pay laws apply to employers with one or more employees

State Laws Prohibiting Discrimination in Employment, con't

Private employers may not make employment decisions based on

Gender	Marital status	Pregnancy, childbirth, and related medical conditions	Race or color	Religion or creed	Sexual orientation	Genetic testing information	Additional protected categories
✓			✓	✓		✓	• Preexisting injury
✓			✓	✓			• Refer to chart on Family and Medical Leave
✓		✓	✓	✓		✓	
✓		✓	✓	✓			
✓			✓	✓	✓	✓	• Place of birth
✓	✓	✓	✓	✓		✓	
✓	✓	✓	✓	✓		✓	• Hepatitis C infection • Member of state militia
✓4			✓	✓			• Smoking away from work
✓	✓	✓	✓	✓	✓	✓	• Arrest or conviction • Lawful use of any product when not at work • Military service or status
✓			✓	✓			• Military service or status • Smoking off duty

Current as of February 2005

Agencies That Enforce Laws Prohibiting Discrimination in Employment

United States Agencies

Equal Employment Opportunity
Commission (EEOC)
Washington, DC
202-663-4900
800-669-4000
www.eeoc.gov
Field Office locations and phone numbers:
www.eeoc.gov/offices.html

State Agencies

Alabama
EEOC District Office
Birmingham, AL
205-212-2100
205-212-2112
http://eeoc.gov/birmingham/index.html

Alaska
Commission for Human Rights
Anchorage, AK
907-274-4692
800-478-4692
www.gov.state.ak.us/aschr/aschr.htm

Arizona
Civil Rights Division
Phoenix, AZ
602-542-5263
www.attorneygeneral.state.az.us/civil
_rights/index.html

Arkansas
Equal Employment Opportunity
Commission
Little Rock, AR
501-324-5060
www.eeoc.gov/littlerock/index.html

California
Department of Fair Employment and
Housing
Sacramento District Office
Sacramento, CA
916-445-5523
800-884-1684
www.dfeh.ca.gov

Colorado
Civil Rights Division
Denver, CO
303-894-2997
800-262-4845
www.dora.state.co.us/Civil-Rights

Connecticut
Commission on Human Rights and
Opportunities
Hartford, CT
860-541-3400
800-477-5737
www.state.ct.us/chro

Delaware
Office of Labor Law Enforcement
Division of Industrial Affairs
Wilmington, DE
302-761-8200
www.delawareworks.com/industrialaffairs/
welcome.shtml

District of Columbia
Office of Human Rights
Washington, DC
202-727-4559
http://ohr.dc.gov/ohr/site/default.asp

Florida
Commission on Human Relations
Tallahassee, FL
850-488-7082
800-342-8170
http://fchr.state.fl.us

Georgia
Atlanta District Office
U.S. Equal Employment Opportunity
Commission
Atlanta, GA
404-562-6800
800-669-4000
www.eeoc.gov/atlanta/index.html

Hawaii
Hawai'i Civil Rights Commission
Honolulu, HI
808-586-8636 (Oahu only)
800-468-4644 x68636 (other islands)
http://dlir.state.hi.us/divisions/hcrc

Idaho
Idaho Commission on Human Rights
Boise, ID
208-334-2873
www2.state.id.us/ihrc

Illinois
Department of Human Rights
Chicago, IL
312-814-6200
www.state.il.us/dhr

Indiana
Civil Rights Commission
Indianapolis, IN
317-232-2600
800-628-2909
www.in.gov/icrc

Iowa
Iowa Civil Rights Commission
Des Moines, IA
515-281-4121
800-457-4416
www.state.ia.us/government/crc

Kansas
Human Rights Commission
Topeka, KS
785-296-3206
www.ink.org/public/khrc

Kentucky
Human Rights Commission
Louisville, KY
502-595-4024
800-292-5566
www.state.ky.us/agencies2/kchr

Louisiana
Commission on Human Rights
Baton Rouge, LA
225-342-6969

Maine
Human Rights Commission
Augusta, ME
207-624-6050
www.state.me.us/mhrc/index.shtml

Maryland
Commission on Human Relations
Baltimore, MD
410-767-8600
800-637-6247
www.mchr.state.md.us

Massachusetts
Commission Against Discrimination
Boston, MA
617-994-6000
www.state.ma.us/mcad

Michigan
Department of Civil Rights
Detroit, MI
313-456-3700
800-482-3604
www.michigan.gov/mdcr

Minnesota
Department of Human Rights
St. Paul, MN
651-296-5663
800-657-3704
www.humanrights.state.mn.us

Mississippi
Equal Opportunity Department
Employment Security Commission
Jackson, MS
601-961-7420
www.mesc.state.ms.us

Missouri
Commission on Human Rights
Jefferson City, MO
573-751-3325
www.dolir.state.mo.us/hr

Montana
Human Rights Bureau
Employment Relations Division
Department of Labor and Industry
Helena, MT
406-444-2884
800-542-0807
http://erd.dli.state.mt.us/HumanRight/
HRhome.asp

Nebraska
Equal Opportunity Commission
Lincoln, NE
402-471-2024
800-642-6112
www.nol.org/home/NEOC

Nevada
Equal Rights Commission
Reno, NV
775-688-1288
http://detr.state.nv.us/nerc/NERC-index.htm

New Hampshire
Commission for Human Rights
Concord, NH
603-271-2767
http://webster.state.nh.us/hrc

New Jersey
Division on Civil Rights
Newark, NJ
973-648-2700
www.state.nj.us/lps/dcr

New Mexico
Human Rights Division
Santa Fe, NM
505-827-6838
800-566-9471
www.dol.state.nm.us/dol_hrd.html

New York
Division of Human Rights
Bronx, NY
718-741-8400
www.nysdhr.com

North Carolina
Employment Discrimination Bureau
Department of Labor
Raleigh, NC
919-807-2796
800-NCLABOR (625-2267)
www.dol.state.nc.us/edb/edb.htm

North Dakota
Human Rights Division
Department of Labor
Bismarck, ND
701-328-2660
800-582-8032
www.state.nd.us/labor/services/human-rights

Ohio
Civil Rights Commission
Columbus, OH
614-466-5928
888-278-7101
www.state.oh.us/crc

Oklahoma
Human Rights Commission
Oklahoma City, OK
405-521-2360
www.youroklahoma.com/ohrc

Oregon
Civil Rights Division
Bureau of Labor and Industries
Portland, OR
503-731-4874
www.boli.state.or.us/BOLI/CRD/index.shtml

Pennsylvania
Human Relations Commission
Philadelphia, PA
215-560-2496
www.phrc.state.pa.us

Rhode Island
Commission for Human Rights
Providence, RI
401-222-2661
www.state.ri.us/manual/data/queries
/stdept_.idc?id=16

South Carolina
Human Affairs Commission
Columbia, SC
803-737-7800
800-521-0725
www.state.sc.us/schac

South Dakota
Division of Human Rights
Pierre, SD
605-773-4493
www.state.sd.us/dcr/hr/HR_HOM.htm

Tennessee
Human Rights Commission
Knoxville, TN
865-594-6500
800-251-3589
www.state.tn.us/humanrights

Texas
Commission on Human Rights
Austin, TX
512-437-3450
888-452-4778
http://tchr.state.tx.us

Utah
Anti-Discrimination and Labor Division
Labor Commission
Salt Lake City, UT
801-530-6801
800-222-1238

http://laborcommission.utah.gov/Utah_
Antidiscrimination
___Labo/utah_antidiscrimination___labo.htm

Vermont
Attorney General's Office
Civil Rights Division
Montpelier, VT
802-828-3171
888-745-9195
www.state.vt.us/atg/civil rights.htm

Virginia
Council on Human Rights
Richmond, VA
804-225-2292
www.chr.state.va.us

Washington
Human Rights Commission
Seattle, WA
206-464-6500
www.wa.gov/hrc

West Virginia
Human Rights Commission
Charleston, WV
304-558-2616
888-676-5546
www.wvf.state.wv.us/wvhrc

Wisconsin
Department of Workforce Development
Madison, WI
608-266-6860
www.dwd.state.wi.us/er

Wyoming
Department of Employment
Cheyenne, WY
307-777-7261
http://wydoe.state.wy.us/doe.asp?ID=3

Current as of February 2005

Departments of Labor

U.S. Department of Labor

Washington, DC 20210
202-693-4650
www.dol.gov
You can find a list of regional offices
of the Wage and Hour Division at the
Department of Labor's website at:
www.dol.gov/esa/contacts/whd/america2.htm
and a comprehensive list of state labor
resources at: www.dol.gov/dol/location.htm.

State Labor Departments

Note: Phone numbers are for department
headquarters. Check websites for regional
office locations and numbers.

Alabama

Department of Industrial Relations
Montgomery, AL
334-242-8990
www.dir.state.al.us

Alaska

Department of Labor and Workforce
Development
Juneau, AK
907-465-2700
www.labor.state.ak.us

Arizona

Industrial Commission
Phoenix, AZ
602-542-4411
www.ica.state.az.us

Arkansas

Department of Labor
Little Rock, AR
501-682-4541
www.state.ar.us/labor

California

Department of Industrial Relations
San Francisco, CA
415-703-5050
www.dir.ca.gov

Colorado

Department of Labor and Employment
Denver, CO
303-318-8000
www.coworkforce.com

Connecticut

Labor Department
Wethersfield, CT
860-263-6505
www.ctdol.state.ct.us

Delaware

Department of Labor
Wilmington, DE
302-761-8000
www.delawareworks.com

District of Columbia

Department of Employment Services
Washington, DC
202-671-1900
http://does.ci.washington.dc.us

Florida

Agency for Workforce Innovation
Tallahassee, FL
850-245-7105
www.floridajobs.org or www.MyFlorida
.com

Georgia

Department of Labor
Atlanta, GA
404-656-3011
877-709-8185
www.dol.state.ga.us

Hawaii
Department of Labor and Industrial
Relations
Honolulu, HI
808-586-8865/8844
http://dlir.state.hi.us

Idaho
Department of Labor
Boise, ID
208-334-6112
www.labor.state.id.us

Illinois
Department of Labor
Chicago, IL
312-793-2800
www.state.il.us/agency/idol

Indiana
Department of Labor
Indianapolis, IN
317-232-2655
www.in.gov/labor

Iowa
Iowa Workforce Development
Des Moines, IA
515-281-5387
800-JOB-IOWA
www.iowaworkforce.org/labor

Kansas
Department of Human Resources
Office of Employment Standards
Topeka, KS
785-296-4062
www.dol.ks.gov

Kentucky
Department of Labor
Frankfort, KY
502-564-3070
www.kylabor.net

Louisiana
Department of Labor
Baton Rouge, LA
225-342-3111
www.ldol.state.la.us

Maine
Department of Labor
Augusta, ME
207-287-3787
www.state.me.us/labor

Maryland
Department of Labor, Licensing, and
Regulation
Division of Labor and Industry
Baltimore, MD
410-767-2236
www.dllr.state.md.us/labor

Massachusetts
Department of Labor and Workforce
Development
Boston, MA
617-727-6573
www.state.ma.us/dlwd *or* www.mass.gov/
dlwd

Michigan
Department of Labor and Economic
Growth
Lansing, MI
517-373-3034
www.cis.state.mi.us *or* www.michigan
.gov/cis

Minnesota
Department of Labor and Industry
St. Paul, MN
651-284-5005
800-342-5354
www.doli.state.mn.us

Mississippi
Department of Employment Security
Jackson, MS
601-321-6100
www.mesc.state.ms.us

Missouri
Department of Labor and Industrial
Relations
Jefferson City, MO
573-751-4091
573-751-9691
www.dolir.state.mo.us or www.dolir.mo.gov

Montana
Department of Labor and Industry
Helena, MT
406-444-2840
http://dli.state.mt.us

Nebraska
Department of Labor
Labor and Safety Standards
Lincoln, NE
402-471-2239

Omaha, NE
402-595-3095
www.dol.state.ne.us

Nevada
Division of Industrial Relations
Carson City, NV
775-684-7260
http://dirweb.state.nv.us

New Hampshire
Department of Labor
Concord, NH
603-271-3176
www.labor.state.nh.us

New Jersey
Department of Labor
Labor Standards and Safety Enforcement
Trenton, NJ
609-292-2313/2323
www.state.nj.us/labor

New Mexico
Labor and Industrial Division
Department of Labor
Santa Fe, NM
505-827-6875

Albuquerque, NM
505-841-8993
www.dol.state.nm.us

New York
Department of Labor
Albany, NY
518-457-9000
www.labor.state.ny.us

North Carolina
Department of Labor
Raleigh, NC
919-807-2796
800-625-2267
www.dol.state.nc.us or www.nclabor.com

North Dakota
Department of Labor
Bismarck, ND
701-328-2660
800-582-8032
www.state.nd.us/labor

Ohio
Division of Labor and Worker Safety
Department of Commerce
Columbus, OH
614-644-2239
www.com.state.oh.us/ODOC/laws/default
.htm

Oklahoma
Department of Labor
Oklahoma City, OK
405-528-1500, ext. 200
888-269-5353
www.okdol.state.ok.us or www.ok.gov

Oregon
Bureau of Labor and Industries
Portland, OR
503-731-4200
www.boli.state.or.us

Pennsylvania
Department of Labor and Industry
Harrisburg, PA
717-787-5279
www.dli.state.pa.us

Rhode Island
Department of Labor and Training
Cranston, RI
401-462-8000
www.dlt.state.ri.us *or* www.det.state.ri.us

South Carolina
Department of Labor, Licensing, and
Regulation
Columbia, SC
803-896-4300
www.llr.state.sc.us

South Dakota
Division of Labor and Management
Pierre, SD
605-773-3681
www.state.sd.us/dol/dlm/dlm-home.htm

Tennessee
Department of Labor and Workforce
Development
Nashville, TN
615-741-6642
www.state.tn.us/labor-wfd

Texas
Texas Workforce Commission
Austin, TX
512-463-2222
www.twc.state.tx.us

Utah
Labor Commission
Salt Lake City, UT
801-530-6801
800-222-1238
www.labor.state.ut.us

Vermont
Department of Labor and Industry
Montpelier, VT
808-828-2288
www.state.vt.us/labind

Virginia
Department of Labor and Industry
Richmond, VA
804-371-2327
www.dli.state.va.us

Washington
Department of Labor and Industries
Olympia, WA
360-902-5800
800-547-8367
www.lni.wa.gov

West Virginia
Division of Labor
Charleston, WV
877-558-5134
304-558-7890
www.labor.state.wv.us

Wisconsin
Department of Workforce Development
Madison, WI
608-266-3131
www.dwd.state.wi.us

Wyoming
Department of Employment
Cheyenne, WY
307-777-6763
http://wydoe.state.wy.us

Current as of February 2005 ■

Index

CATALOG

...more from nolo

	PRICE	CODE
BUSINESS		
Becoming a Mediator: Your Guide to Career Opportunities	$29.99	BECM
Business Buyout Agreements (Book w/CD-ROM)	$49.99	BSAG
The CA Nonprofit Corporation Kit (Binder w/CD-ROM)	$69.99	CNP
California Workers' Comp: How to Take Charge		
When You're Injured on the Job	$34.99	WORK
The Complete Guide to Buying a Business	$24.99	BUYBU
The Complete Guide to Selling Your Business	$24.99	SELBU
Consultant & Independent Contractor Agreements (Book w/CD-ROM)	$29.99	CICA
The Corporate Records Handbook (Book w/CD-ROM)	$69.99	CORMI
Create Your Own Employee Handbook (Book w/CD-ROM)	$49.99	EMHA
Dealing With Problem Employees	$44.99	PROBM
Deduct It! Lower Your Small Business Taxes	$34.99	DEDU
Effective Fundraising for Nonprofits	$24.99	EFFN
The Employer's Legal Handbook	$39.99	EMPL
Federal Employment Laws	$49.99	FELW
Form Your Own Limited Liability Company (Book w/CD-ROM)	$44.99	LIAB
Home Business Deductions: Keep What You Earn	$34.99	DEHB
How to Create a Noncompete Agreement (Book w/CD-ROM)	$44.95	NOCMP
How to Form a California Professional Corporation (Book w/CD-ROM)	$59.99	PROF
How to Form a Nonprofit Corporation (Book w/CD-ROM)—National Edition	$49.99	NNP
How to Form a Nonprofit Corporation in California (Book w/CD-ROM)	$49.99	NON
How to Form Your Own California Corporation (Binder w/CD-ROM)	$59.99	CACI
How to Form Your Own California Corporation (Book w/CD-ROM)	$34.99	CCOR
How to Get Your Business on the Web	$29.99	WEBS
How to Run a Thriving Business: Strategies for Success & Satisfaction	$19.99	THRV

Prices subject to change.

ORDER 24 HOURS A DAY @ www.nolo.com
Call 800-728-3555 • Mail or fax the order form in this book

	PRICE	CODE
How to Write a Business Plan	$34.99	SBS
Incorporate Your Business	$49.99	NIBS
The Independent Paralegal's Handbook	$34.99	PARA
Legal Guide for Starting & Running a Small Business	$34.99	RUNS
Legal Forms for Starting & Running a Small Business (Book w/CD-ROM)	$29.99	RUNSF
LLC or Corporation?	$24.99	CHENT
The Manager's Legal Handbook	$39.99	ELBA
Marketing Without Advertising	$20.00	MWAD
Mediate, Don't Litigate	$24.99	MEDL
Music Law (Book w/CD-ROM)	$39.99	ML
Negotiate the Best Lease for Your Business	$24.99	LESP
Nolo's Guide to Social Security Disability	$29.99	QSS
Nolo's Quick LLC	$29.99	LLCQ
Nondisclosure Agreements (Book w/CD-ROM)	$39.95	NAG
The Partnership Book: How to Write a Partnership Agreement (Book w/CD-ROM)	$39.99	PART
The Performance Appraisal Handbook	$29.99	PERF
The Small Business Start-up Kit (Book w/CD-ROM)	$24.99	SMBU
The Small Business Start-up Kit for California (Book w/CD-ROM)	$24.99	OPEN
Starting & Running a Successful Newsletter or Magazine	$29.99	MAG
Tax Savvy for Small Business	$36.99	SAVVY
Workplace Investigations: A Step by Step Legal Guide	$39.99	CMPLN
Working for Yourself: Law & Taxes for Independent Contractors, Freelancers & Consultants	$39.99	WAGE
Working With Independent Contractors (Book w/CD-ROM)	$29.99	HICI
Your Crafts Business: A Legal Guide (Book w/CD-ROM)	$26.99	VART
Your Limited Liability Company: An Operating Manual (Book w/CD-ROM)	$49.99	LOP
Your Rights in the Workplace	$29.99	YRW

	PRICE	CODE

CONSUMER

How to Win Your Personal Injury Claim	$29.99	PICL
Nolo's Encyclopedia of Everyday Law	$29.99	EVL
Nolo's Guide to California Law	$24.99	CLAW

ESTATE PLANNING & PROBATE

8 Ways to Avoid Probate	$19.99	PRAV
Estate Planning Basics	$21.99	ESPN
The Executor's Guide: Settling a Loved One's Estate or Trust	$34.99	EXEC
How to Probate an Estate in California	$49.99	PAE
Make Your Own Living Trust (Book w/CD-ROM)	$39.99	LITR
Nolo's Simple Will Book (Book w/CD-ROM)	$36.99	SWIL
Plan Your Estate	$44.99	NEST
Quick & Legal Will Book	$16.99	QUIC
Quicken Willmaker: Estate Planning Essentials (Book with Interactive CD-ROM)	$49.99	QWMB
Special Needs Trust: Protect Your Child's Financial Future	$34.99	SPNT

FAMILY MATTERS

Building a Parenting Agreement That Works	$24.99	CUST
The Complete IEP Guide	$34.99	IEP
Divorce & Money: How to Make the Best Financial Decisions During Divorce	$34.99	DIMO
Do Your Own California Adoption: Nolo's Guide for Stepparents and Domestic Partners (Book w/CD-ROM)	$34.99	ADOP
Every Dog's Legal Guide: A Must-Have book for Your Owner	$19.99	DOG
Get a Life: You Don't Need a Million to Retire Well	$24.99	LIFE
The Guardianship Book for California	$34.99	GB
A Legal Guide for Lesbian and Gay Couples	$34.99	LG
Living Together: A Legal Guide (Book w/CD-ROM)	$34.99	LTK
Living Wills and Powers of Attorney in California (Book w/CD-ROM)	$21.99	CPOA

	PRICE	CODE
Nolo's IEP Guide: Learning Disabilities	$29.99	IELD
Prenuptial Agreements: How to Write a		
Fair & Lasting Contract (Book w/CD-ROM)	$34.99	PNUP
Using Divorce Mediation: Save Your Money & Your Sanity	$29.99	UDMD

GOING TO COURT

	PRICE	CODE
Beat Your Ticket: Go To Court & Win! (National Edition)	$21.99	BEYT
The Criminal Law Handbook: Know Your Rights, Survive the System	$34.99	KYR
Everybody's Guide to Small Claims Court (National Edition)	$26.99	NSCC
Everybody's Guide to Small Claims Court in California	$29.99	CSCC
Fight Your Ticket & Win in California	$29.99	FYT
How to Change Your Name in California..	$34.99	NAME
How to Collect When You Win a Lawsuit (California Edition)	$29.99	JUDG
The Lawsuit Survival Guide	$29.99	UNCL
Nolo's Deposition Handbook	$29.99	DEP
Represent Yourself in Court: How to Prepare & Try a Winning Case	$34.99	RYC
Win Your Lawsuit: A Judge's Guide to Representing Yourself		
in CA Superior Court	$29.99	SLWY

HOMEOWNERS, LANDLORDS & TENANTS

	PRICE	CODE
California Tenants' Rights	$27.99	CTEN
Deeds for California Real Estate	$24.99	DEED
Every Landlord's Legal Guide (National Edition, Book w/CD-ROM)	$34.99	ELLI
Every Landlord's Tax Deduction Guide	$44.99	DELL
Every Tenant's Legal Guide	$29.99	EVTEN
For Sale by Owner in California	$29.99	FSBO
How to Buy a House in California	$34.99	BHCA
The California Landlord's Law Book: Rights & Responsibilities		
(Book w/CD-ROM)	$44.99	LBRT

	PRICE	CODE
The California Landlord's Law Book: Evictions (Book w/CD-ROM)	$44.99	LBEV
Leases & Rental Agreements	$29.99	LEAR
Neighbor Law: Fences, Trees, Boundaries & Noise	$26.99	NEI
The New York Landlord's Law Book (Book w/CD-ROM)	$39.99	NYLL
New York Tenants' Rights	$27.99	NYTEN
Renters' Rights (National Edition)	$24.99	RENT

IMMIGRATION

	PRICE	CODE
Becoming a U.S. Citizen: A Guide to the Law, Exam and Interview	$24.99	USCIT
Fiancé & Marriage Visas (Book w/CD-ROM)	$44.95	IMAR
How to Get a Green Card	$29.99	GRN
Student & Tourist Visas	$29.95	ISTU
U.S. Immigration Made Easy	$44.99	IMEZ

MONEY MATTERS

	PRICE	CODE
101 Law Forms for Personal Use (Book w/CD-ROM)	$29.99	SPOT
Bankruptcy: Is It the Right Solution to Your Debt Problems?	$21.99	BRS
Chapter 13 Bankruptcy: Repay Your Debts	$36.99	CHB
Credit Repair (Book w/CD-ROM)	$24.99	CREP
Getting Paid: How to Collect from Bankrupt Debtors	$29.99	CRBNK
How to File for Chapter 7 Bankruptcy	$29.99	HFB
IRAs, 401(k)s & Other Retirement Plans: Taking Your Money Out	$34.99	RET
Solve Your Money Troubles	$29.99	MT
Stand Up to the IRS	$29.99	SIRS
Surviving an IRS Tax Audit	$24.95	SAUD
Take Control of Your Student Loan Debt	$26.95	SLOAN

PATENTS AND COPYRIGHTS

	PRICE	CODE
All I need is Money: How To Finance Your Invention	$19.99	FINA

	PRICE	CODE
The Copyright Handbook: How to Protect and Use Written Works (Book w/CD-ROM)	$39.99	COHA
Copyright Your Software (Book w/CD-ROM)	$34.95	CYS
Getting Permission: How to License and Clear Copyrighted Materials Online and Off (Book w/CD-ROM)	$34.99	RIPER
How to Make Patent Drawings	$29.99	DRAW
The Inventor's Notebook	$24.99	INOT
License Your Invention (Book w/CD-ROM)	$39.99	LICE
Nolo's Patents for Beginners	$29.99	QPAT
Patenting Art & Entertainment: New Strategies for Protecting Creative Ideas	$39.99	PATAE
Patent, Copyright & Trademark	$39.99	PCTM
Patent It Yourself	$49.99	PAT
Patent Pending in 24 Hours	$29.99	PEND
The Public Domain	$34.95	PUBL
Trademark: Legal Care for Your Business and Product Name	$39.99	TRD
Web and Software Development: A Legal Guide (Book w/ CD-ROM)	$44.99	SFT
What Every Inventor Needs to Know About Business and Taxes (Book w/CD-ROM)	$21.99	ILAX

RESEARCH & REFERENCE

	PRICE	CODE
Legal Research: How to Find & Understand the Law	$39.99	LRES

SENIORS

	PRICE	CODE
Long-Term Care: How to Plan & Pay for It	$19.99	ELD
Social Security, Medicare & Government Pensions	$29.99	SOA

SOFTWARE
Call or check our website at www.nolo.com
for special discounts on Software!

Incorporator Pro $89.99   STNC1

LLC Maker—Windows $89.95   LLP1

Patent Pending Now! $19.99   PP1

PatentEase—Windows .... $349.00   PEAS

Personal RecordKeeper 5.0 CD—Windows $59.95   RKD5

Quicken Legal Business Pro 2006—Windows $109.99   SBQB6

Quicken WillMaker Plus 2006—Windows $79.99   WQP6

SPECIAL UPGRADE OFFER
Get 35% off the latest edition of your Nolo book

It's important to have the most current legal information. Because laws and legal procedures change often, we update our books regularly. To help keep you up-to-date we are extending this special upgrade offer. Cut out and mail the title portion of the cover of your old Nolo book and we'll give you 35% off the retail price of the NEW EDITION of that book when you purchase directly from us. For more information call us at 1-800-728-3555. This offer is to individuals only.

Order Form

Name _____

Address _____

City _____

State, Zip _____

Daytime Phone _____

E-mail _____

Item Code	Quantity	Item	Unit Price	Total Price

Method of payment

☐ Check   ☐ VISA   ☐ MasterCard

☐ Discover Card   ☐ American Express

Subtotal	
Add your local sales tax (California only)	
Shipping: RUSH $12, Basic $9 (See below)	
"I bought 3, ship it to me FREE!"(Ground shipping only)	
TOTAL	

Account Number _____

Expiration Date _____

Signature _____

Shipping and Handling

Rush Delivery—Only $12

We'll ship any order to any street address in the U.S. by UPS 2nd Day Air* for only $12!

* Order by noon Pacific Time and get your order in 2 business days. Orders placed after noon Pacific Time will arrive in 3 business days. P.O. boxes and S.F. Bay Area use basic shipping. Alaska and Hawaii use 2nd Day Air or Priority Mail.

Basic Shipping—$9

Use for P.O. Boxes, Northern California and Ground Service.

Allow 1-2 weeks for delivery. U.S. addresses only.

For faster service, use your credit card and our toll-free numbers

Call our customer service group
Monday thru Friday 7am to 7pm PST

Phone	1-800-728-3555
Fax	1-800-645-0895
Mail	Nolo
	950 Parker St.
	Berkeley, CA 94710

Order 24 hours a day @
www.nolo.com

Remember:

Little publishers have big ears.
We really listen to you.

Take 2 Minutes & Give Us Your 2 cents

Your comments make a big difference in the development and revision of Nolo books and software. Please take a few minutes and register your Nolo product—and your comments—with us. Not only will your input make a difference, you'll receive special offers available only to registered owners of Nolo products on our newest books and software. Register now by:

PHONE
1-800-728-3555

FAX
1-800-645-0895

EMAIL
cs@nolo.com

or **MAIL** us
this registration card

fold here

- -

NOLO Registration Card

NAME _____ DATE _____

ADDRESS _____

_____

CITY _____ STATE _____ ZIP _____

PHONE _____ EMAIL _____

WHERE DID YOU HEAR ABOUT THIS PRODUCT? _____

WHERE DID YOU PURCHASE THIS PRODUCT? _____

DID YOU CONSULT A LAWYER? (PLEASE CIRCLE ONE)   YES   NO   NOT APPLICABLE

DID YOU FIND THIS BOOK HELPFUL?   (VERY)   5   4   3   2   1   (NOT AT ALL)

COMMENTS _____

_____

_____

WAS IT EASY TO USE?   (VERY EASY)   5   4   3   2   1   (VERY DIFFICULT)

We occasionally make our mailing list available to carefully selected companies whose products may be of interest to you.

☐ If you do not wish to receive mailings from these companies, please check this box.

☐ You can quote me in future Nolo promotional materials.
   Daytime phone number _____.

JOB 1.0

Nolo in the NEWS

"Nolo helps lay people perform legal tasks without the aid—or fees—of lawyers."

—USA TODAY

Nolo books are ...*"written in plain language, free of legal mumbo jumbo, and spiced with witty personal observations."*

—ASSOCIATED PRESS

"...Nolo publications...guide people simply through the how, when, where and why of law."

—WASHINGTON POST

"Increasingly, people who are not lawyers are performing tasks usually regarded as legal work... And consumers, using books like Nolo's, do routine legal work themselves."

—NEW YORK TIMES

"...All of [Nolo's] books are easy-to-understand, are updated regularly, provide pull-out forms...and are often quite moving in their sense of compassion for the struggles of the lay reader."

—SAN FRANCISCO CHRONICLE

- - - - - - - - - - - - - - - - - - - fold here -

Nolo
950 Parker Street
Berkeley, CA 94710-9867

Attn: JOB 1.0